Historians in the Middle Ages

Historians
in the Middle Ages

BERYL SMALLEY

with 99 illustrations, 10 in colour

THAMES AND HUDSON · LONDON

1 Frontispiece: Clio, Muse of History. Medieval scholars had a literary knowledge of the Nine Muses from their reading of Latin classical texts. From a Roman sarcophagus showing the Muses. *Paris, Louvre*

Picture research: Georgina Bruckner

Filmset and printed in Great Britain by BAS Printers Limited, Wallop, Hampshire

Contents

For my friends at Berkeley, California

Foreword

This book has been written with the aim of helping students and general readers to read medieval histories and chronicles with pleasure. I shall use the word 'historiography' as a blanket term to signify historical writings, because medieval authors distinguished between various genres: 'history' meant one thing, 'chronicle' another, and both differed from the several forms that biography might take. The history of historiography is a rather new subject. Modern historians used to read medieval historiographers as sources for facts, opinions and attitudes; we still do. But now Crocè and his pupils have put the history of historiography on the academic map. We also try to find out what medieval writers aimed at as historiographers and how the art and skill of historiography developed through the ages.

First we need to know something about the material conditions they worked in, secondly what books they read and how their reading formed their minds as historiographers. In describing the historiographers I have had to select ruthlessly. Many old favourites have been left out. I have kept mainly to Latin historiography within the area bounded roughly by the North Sea, the Pyrenees and Naples, with one excursion into Poland (my pupil Mr B. Harónski introduced me to Master Vincent of Cracow). Crusading historiography falls into the area, since the Latin kingdom in Palestine was a colony known as 'France Overseas'. I have excluded autobiography and hagiography, the writing of the lives and passions of saints. Medieval autobiographies are rare and untypical; lives of saints on the other hand are so numerous that they would need a book to themselves. I hope to convey some idea of the bewildering richness and variety of medieval historiography. Specialists may think that I pay too much attention to the freaks; but the student can correct me by browsing in run-of-the-mill chronicles and annals. My freaks and the great artists and thinkers may perhaps whet his appetite for the ordinary.

ꓫSꓤ· ꓩᴅᴑꓤ·   ᴇꓤ·ᴠ·ꓔꓯ·ᴑꓤ

ᴇᴀᴄ·ᴍᴘᴀˑꓒꓴ·ꓲ·ꓒꓯ·ꓲˑ
ᴍᴄꓴᴇꓲ·ꓯ·ᴍᴘꓯ·ꓲ·ᴍᴘᴀ·ꓲᴄ·ᴇꓲ

ꓒꓲꓚ·ᴇ·ᴄ·ꓲ

ꓢᴄꓤꓲꓒꓔꓳꓤꓲꓢ·ꓟꓲꓢᴇꓤꓲ·ꓒꓲꓰꓓꓯꓤᴇ·ꓒꓢ·ꓟꓲꓢᴄᴇꓤꓲ·ꓢꓳꓲꓛᴄꓴꓡꓒꓯꓤꓴ·   ꓒꓳꓠꓒꓒᴇꓠꓢꓯꓤᴇ·ꓟᴇꓯꓤꓴ
ꓒꓯꓤꓴꓯꓓꓲꓛᴇꓡ·ꓐꓳꓠꓯꓢꓲꓠ·ꓢꓴ·ꓑ·ᴇꓤꓯꓡꓲꓟꓯꓟꓯꓡꓲ·ꓢꓲꓲ·ꓠꓳꓠ·ꓡꓴᴄꓲᴄᴇꓒꓯꓔ·ꓴꓲꓡꓰ·ꓟꓳꓤꓢ

ꓲꓢꓔᴇ·ꓤᴇ·   ᴄꓒꓠꓲ

The conditions

What motives led men to write histories and chronicles in the Middle Ages? Answers will emerge in the course of this book. To prevent misunderstanding, I shall begin by excluding motives which we take for granted nowadays. Today historiography is commercialized. A textbook or pot-boiler pays for a holiday or adds to one's income; a work of scholarship helps the author to compete for posts in the job market. Enjoyment and compulsion to write come into it; but the day of the amateur scholar is past. There was no money in authorship in the Middle Ages.

The history of book production in the ancient world shows that the author made no direct profit even then, although he could count on a reading public of aristocrats and bourgeois. Publishers and booksellers existed in ancient times and earned their living in ancient cities; but the copying of books was too costly to admit of profit-sharing. A rich author would dictate his book to a slave skilled at the job. He then had it copied and circulated at his own expense. The poorer author would hand his book to a publisher, who might pay him a small sum for the manuscript; more likely he would have to pay something himself. Copyright and royalties were out of the question. A book belonged to its author for as long as it stayed in his hands. After that it was free as air. A plagiarist laid himself open to mockery and reproach – if his fraud was discovered; the victim had no legal remedy. Authors might hope for indirect reward in the form of patronage, since wealthy men of rank liked to have talented writers in their clientèle. Patronage, however, had the drawback of being precarious and degrading. The typical historian of the ancient world was a retired statesman of independent means who had left public life in disgrace or under a cloud, and then devoted himself to writing as an honourable activity in his enforced leisure. Sometimes his history took the form of memoirs; sometimes he chose a more remote period. In either case he wrote because he was rich already, not to make money. Sallust, Tacitus and the Jewish historian Flavius

2 Opposite: a monk copyist receives a supernatural reward. At the lower right he is shown lying dead, while an angel carries his soul in the form of a child to be judged by God. His good deeds are weighed in the judgment scales. The book he has copied, and to which this picture forms the frontispiece, weighs heavily in his favour. Above at the left we see St Isidore of Seville, whose *Etymologies* the monk has copied (see p. 22). The manuscript was produced at Regensburg in the midtwelfth century. *Munich, Bayerische Staatsbibliothek, Cod. lat. 13031, f.1r*

3 Stages of book production in a monastic scriptorium. The skin is stretched on a frame and scraped with a knife to clean and smooth it (top). Then it is cut into quires. Finally, the gatherings are stitched together. From a copy of the works of St Ambrose made at Bamberg in the first half of the twelfth century. *Bamberg, Staatsbibliothek, MS Patr. 5, f.1v*

Josephus are examples. The cult of 'good fame', an indirect reward for his pains, supplied the driving motive for an ancient historian.

In the Middle Ages, between about 800 and 1200, the expenses of book production increased. The ancient papyrus roll had given way to costly parchment or vellum, prepared as quires and stitched together. They needed a hard cover to keep them from falling apart. Skilled slave-labour for copying was no longer available; the ancient bookshop had vanished. The book itself was now a precious object. It circulated as a gift or medium of exchange or as an extravagant purchase. The main centres of book production were now *scriptoria*, or writing offices, in monasteries and cathedrals. The monks or canons would sometimes employ professional scribes or artists; they often did the work of copying and illuminating themselves. The demand for books had shrunk, since the literate layman had become a rarity; readers were mainly churchmen. Court patronage survived; but most authors wrote to order or with the permission of an ecclesiastical superior rather than to please a secular prince. Historiography continued to be a spare-time occupation. The personal incentive had decreased. Christian humility forbad that the author should write in order to boost his good fame. Indeed the whole concept of authorship went by the board. An 'author' in medieval terms means 'authority'. The biblical writers and the Church Fathers ranked as 'authors' in sacred literature; the classical poets and prose-writers were their opposite numbers in profane literature. Their successors in the Middle Ages counted as mere 'writers' or 'compilers', who lacked the weight of 'authority'.

Plagiarism moved up from the vices to the virtues: one should never put in one's own weak words what had been said better already. A historiographer recording contemporary events found himself forced to be original to some extent. He tells us so and apologizes. The changed attitude to authorship put a premium on anonymity. The writer preferred not to give his name, or else he sheltered under some greater name of the past. Hence the crop of 'anonymous' and 'pseudo' authors in books on medieval thought and learning. Forgery joined plagiarism in the ranks of the virtues.

The thirteenth and fourteenth centuries saw a revolution in book production. It catered for an increased demand. More people could read and had time to read. The invention of spectacles in about 1300 prolonged reading capacity into

old age. The publisher or 'stationer' reappeared, especially in university towns. He paid professionals to produce *de luxe* copies to order, but also engaged in mass production for sale in his shop. Labour-saving methods came into use. The volume to be copied was taken apart; the 'pieces', as they were called, would be given out to separate scribes, so that a number could work on the same volume simultaneously. The scribes wrote faster. The process resulted in an uglier type of book, which more customers could afford. Royalties and copyright still had to wait for the invention of printing; but the cost of production went down and the author could reach a wider public than had been possible earlier in the Middle Ages.

The rise of medieval schools and universities brings up the question of the professional profit-motive: a teacher noted as a writer on his subject would attract more pupils. But history was not a teaching subject either in ancient or in medieval times. It was taught as a supplement to other subjects, as we shall see later. No student could enrol himself for a course or be examined in history. The minimal place given to historical works is shown in a booklist drawn up by the university authorities at Paris in 1286. They aimed at protecting masters and students from profiteering by the stationers, and each book on the list is marked with the maximum price to be charged in the shop. The compilers included all texts which masters and students would need as basic reading for their courses. Of some 140 items only three could pass as historical. The first is a compendium of Bible history, with a certain amount of pagan history, made by a

4 Three scribes are shown writing. The middle one holds an inkhorn. From an ivory relief produced in western Germany in the ninth or tenth century, *Vienna, Kunsthistorisches Museum*

Paris master, Peter Comestor, in the late twelfth century and known as the *School History*. It sometimes served as a set text for lectures on theology for beginners. The second item is *Legends of the Saints* and the third is *Lives of the Desert Fathers*. The course in theology included training in preaching and in pastoral care; hence the student needed these items as part of his equipment. Medieval history is wholly lacking, except in so far as *Legends of the Saints* stretched out to cover a few medieval saints, such as Thomas Becket. What a student chose to pay for his spare-time reading was his own business; it did not concern the university.

The history of learning amounts to a history of specialization. One branch of learning after another develops into an autonomous discipline. History was a slow developer. The first chairs in it were founded only in the sixteenth century; in the Middle Ages it was non-profit-making, non-professional and unspecialized.

The way history was presented differed from ours. We think in terms of the written word, or of the mass media for the spoken word. Ancient and medieval writers expected their books to be read aloud. Publication might take the form of reading to a circle of friends or to a larger audience, an ancient practice which was revived in the twelfth century and perhaps earlier. From the very beginning of its composition, the writer had in mind what his book would *sound* like. First, he generally dictated it: pen-driving was a chore to be avoided if help was available. Then he would have it read back to him or read it himself and make corrections. When circulated it would be read aloud. Medieval writers address their audience as 'readers' or 'hearers' interchangeably, and their punctuation often supposes that the text will be read aloud: the text of Orderic Vital's *Ecclesiastical History*, for instance, has symbols to indicate a change of pitch in the reader's voice. Even a person reading 'to himself' pronounced the words aloud and gesticulated as he read. Private reading was therefore regarded as a mental and physical exercise. We do not know, for lack of evidence, just when it became customary to run the eye along the line, relying on the eye alone instead of using both eye and ear. For the moment we have to do with writers who appealed to their public orally. This explains much that we find unfamiliar in medieval historians. A writer who appeals to the ear will try every trick of style at his command to please his audience and keep it on the *qui vive*, whether he addresses it directly or whether he imagines someone else reading aloud. The effect is 'rhetorical' (in our modern, bad sense of the word), as it was meant to be. Eleventh- and twelfth-century historians often use rhythmical prose and drop easily into verse. The most skilful translator of Latin into English cannot avoid clumsiness; the original cadences intended by the writer will not come through in translation.

Direct approach to an audience affected content as well as style. An invisible reader shuts his book with a yawn; an audience shows visible signs of boredom. A ninth-century historian called Agnellus read his history of the Church of his native city, Ravenna, to an audience of clergy and people. He is a warm and chatty person, and he tells us when he breaks off his reading for the day and whether his hearers have been attentive or bored: 'You've been hanging on my words today', or 'Yesterday you showed signs of tedium'. It was all the more pressing to tell lively anecdotes to keep one's hearers amused, as Agnellus does. Modern students are told that they must 'try to get into an author's mind'. To understand a medieval historian they must also sit in his audience. The communication is oral. The author expects them to listen to his periods and to laugh when he makes a joke to amuse them.

The medieval author also assumes that his audience will be familiar with the tradition in which he is working. His predecessors speak through his mouth, and his own reading has conditioned his ideas on what history is and on how it should be written. We need to understand his presuppositions. They go back to antiquity and to the Bible and the Fathers. We shall have to make a long journey backwards in time, to Cicero and Moses, in order to grasp how a medieval historiographer approached his material and how he presented it to his audience. The ancient and Christian traditions intermingled, but it is possible to separate them to some extent when we consider their influence on the writing of history in the Middle Ages. To put it very briefly: Latin antiquity supplied classified genres for the forms that historiography might take, rules for writing in the various genres, and models to be imitated. Medieval authors, in so far as they had a smattering of classical learning, observed or modified the ancient traditions. Their faithfulness to the ancients survived all changes in physical conditions and mental climate. The Bible and the Fathers, on the other hand, influenced the content, scope and purpose of medieval historiography.

2

The Roman legacy

Medieval writers inherited some clear notions about the various genres of historiography. The ancients distinguished between annalists and historians. Annals were records of events, compiled from year to year. A town government would arrange to keep lists of officials, of prizes awarded in the local sports and of treaties or wars with neighbour cities. The annalist set them down for reference purposes and had no reason to present them in literary form. 'Brevity without obscurity' was all he could aim at, according to Cicero. A history differed from annals in being a literary composition. One referred to annals; one read or listened to a history. It took its place beside other literary genres, such as drama or satire. These distinctions were observed in the Middle Ages. Chronicles and annals recorded events in their time sequence, and their compilers did not aim at elegant presentation. The historian by contrast paid attention to style and did not feel bound to a strict chronological order. He could use digressions and flashbacks. He differentiated between history and other literary genres. Two twelfth-century historians, both well read in the Latin classics, give us examples. Otto of Freising in a gloomy moment says that he is writing 'tragedy rather than history'. William of Tyre expresses his disgust at contemporary manners and morals by saying that to describe them would mean writing 'satire rather than history'.

History had a niche in Roman education because it formed part of rhetoric, the most important subject studied and taught in the schools. Rhetoric can be defined as 'the art of persuasion in writing and speech'. The upper-class pupil in a Roman school received the kind of training which would equip him to be an orator, ready to speak in assemblies or in the law courts. As well as learning the technique of public speaking, he would leave his classes equipped with the all-round literary culture suitable to a gentleman. He learned to speak and to write in an elegant style. The art of persuasion includes an appeal to the emotions, and history came into it because a favourite form of appeal was to tell stories by way

5 Opposite: an ancient orator in the dignified pose recommended by Cicero. The art of speech-making or rhetoric was not only a gentleman's accomplishment and a professional asset; it represented the triumph of mind over matter. Virgil compares the calming of a storm by the sea-god Neptune to a grave orator quietening an angry mob (*Aeneid* i, 142–56). History formed part of the study of rhetoric. This is a bronze statuette, probably cast in the first century AD. *London, British Museum*

throughout the changes in facilities for higher education which took place in late antiquity and in the Middle Ages. History was taught in the margin of literature; it was a fringe subject, but safe from extinction as long as the classical, and some of the medieval, poets continued to be studied in the Arts course. The study of the Liberal Arts or *Trivium* comprised grammar, rhetoric and dialectic. The study of history, wedged between grammar and rhetoric, had a minor role in the syllabus. The student would learn the content of ancient history to a greater or lesser extent, but he would not learn how to write history as part of his training in letters. If his master encouraged him to practise his talents in school exercises, these would take the form of verse or prose composition on literary or perhaps on religious themes. We do not hear of school essays on historical subjects as such, though of course a historical episode from ancient or biblical history might serve as a subject for an exercise. The master would 'mark' his pupils according to their skill in literary presentation.

Cicero laid down rules for the orator or 'rhetor' who narrated history. His books on rhetoric made an indelible impression on medieval scholars. First, the narrator of history had a moral responsibility to tell the truth impartially and without malice, even at risk of offending people, since truth might be unpleasant. On method Cicero recommended 'chronological arrangement and geographical representation'. The historian should investigate causes: he should explain not only what great deeds were done, but how they were done and why, estimating the roles of chance and of human wisdom or folly and not forgetting 'lives and characters'. He should write serenely in an easy flowing style. Cicero describes history in terms which flatter its addicts:

History bears witness to the passing of the ages, sheds light upon reality, gives life to recollection and guidance to human existence and brings tidings of ancient days.

A closer look will show that he was cracking up history in order to honour rhetoric. He goes on to ask:

And so, whose voice but the orator's can entrust her to immortality?

His praise gained currency and was quoted by men who may not have read the original. A thirteenth-century annotator of a copy of the *School History*, belonging to the abbey of Jumièges, wrote it into the margin. History was dignified.

8 A thirteenth-century Bolognese teacher of rhetoric, Guido Faba, advertises himself in the foreword to his treatise on the subject, calling students to drink at the well of his wisdom. Two pupils drink from cups. The professor carries two wings on his shoulders (given to him by the archangel St Michael, an event shown in another miniature). One of his wings is to cure faults of style and the other to confer the graces of eloquence on his pupils. The miniature illustrates a textbook called *Rota nova. Oxford, New College, MS 255, f.2v*

Roman historians provided models and examples. The choice of what to read depended partly on taste and partly on the chance survival of manuscripts. Medieval scholars, with rare exceptions, could not read Greek, and they had no translations of the classical Greek historians. Of the Latins, Livy (59 BC–AD 17) was known and admired, but seldom read until he came back into fashion in the late thirteenth century. His *From the Foundation of the City* was too ambitious in scale to serve as a model. Tacitus was not read at all. Sallust (87–36 BC) stands out as the favourite. His *Catiline's Conspiracy* and *Jugurthan War* survived the shrinkage of texts studied in the schools of late antiquity, for they are historical monographs of manageable size. Sallust was valued as a stylist who wrote clear, imitable Latin.

Both the style and the method of Roman historians show the close links between history and rhetoric. There were literary conventions. The historian puts speeches into his characters' mouths: a general addresses his troops before battle, a statesman puts his case in assembly, and so on. Readers are not supposed to take these as tape-recordings or even as an accurate report of what was said: they may represent the gist of it, but their real function is to adorn the style. Medieval students delighted in Sallust's speeches and copied them eagerly. Convention allowed a certain freedom from accuracy. Dates could be dispensed with. Documentation was not called for. The writer would have broken the flow of his eloquence had he inserted copies of edicts and treaties, couched in government language. Cicero's rule that historians must tell the truth did not prescribe the truth in niggling detail.

Sallust treated history as a branch of ethics, which in turn was a branch of rhetoric. The orator was 'a *good* man, skilled in speech'. In theory he ought to use his skill to serve an honourable cause. Sallust had a moral outlook and a moral lesson. The Romans looked back to the old days when their forbears had been soldier-farmers, before prosperity and peace corrupted their descendants and led to civil strife and defeat by foreign enemies. The historian should act as a censor, pointing to good and bad examples. He must discern men's true motives. Sallust was cynical in doing so; he generally believed the worst. His books convinced medieval readers that history was moral and exemplarist in purpose and that the historian had a right both to decorate and to adorn his story. He should mount splendid, dramatic battle

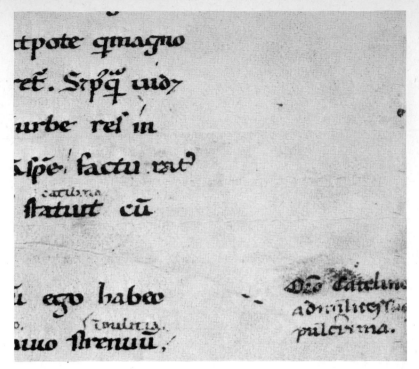

9 Marginal notes to a copy of Sallust's *Catiline Conspiracy* show that it was used as a school text for the study of rhetoric. The note shown here points to 'Catiline's very fine speech to his soldiers', encouraging them to face desperate odds. Medieval historians, mindful of their training in rhetoric, would put quotations from the speeches recorded or invented by Sallust into the mouths of their characters, especially when they described how a general addressed his troops before going into battle. This manuscript was written in the late eleventh or early twelfth century, probably in France. *London, British Museum, MS Harl. 5412, f.17r*

scenes and sieges with set speeches and all the stage properties in his repertoire.

In transmitting samples of the historical monograph, Sallust had a wholesome influence. The genre offered an alternative to the universal history or chronicle on the one hand and local history on the other. His books reinforced by example what Cicero taught on the importance of geography. Sallust described the North African background to the Jugurthan War and explained how it affected the habits and mentality of the Moorish tribes who lived there; he went on to show how these traits accounted for the Moorish victories and final defeat in their wars with Rome. *Catiline's Conspiracy* and *The Jugurthan War* bit so deep into medieval consciousness that borrowings and involuntary memories of Sallustian phrases crop up in literary histories, not to mention imitations of speeches and battle scenes, applied to the story in hand. Julius Caesar wrote a different type of monograph. His *Gallic War* and *Civil War* tell the story of his campaigns in a terse, factual way. Caesar was read and quoted, but less often than Sallust. There was less juice in Caesar; and the monks and clerks who wrote history may have felt closer to a civilian author than they could to a general.

Biography as a genre came down in Suetonius' *Lives of the Caesars* (early second century AD), which began with Julius Caesar and stopped at Domitian. This genre had rules of its own. Suetonius shows us photographs rather than cinema. A *Life* comprises the subject's early career, private life, character, physique and looks, and his public deeds as a ruler. The interaction between public and private did not interest Suetonius, nor did he trace development of character, except to show in some cases that a man might deteriorate under the strain of ruling. He did not go deeply into motive. He could be flippant: according to Suetonius, Julius Caesar decided to invade Britain partly because he was a connoisseur of pearls, which Britain produced in plenty. On moral questions, he refrained from judgment, though he supposed a common standard of right and wrong. He allows that even bad emperors could make good laws and improve judicial procedure.

Not having chosen a rhetorical genre, Suetonius thought it in order to insert record material as evidence. His book *On Grammarians and Rhetors* launched a new type of biography, the lives of literary men. It survived in fragments only, but St Jerome used it as a model for his book *On Illustrious Men*. Hence scholars as well as rulers had a right to biographies. Suetonius caters for readers of all times who say: 'I like history because I'm interested in people.' We should know less about the personal traits of medieval rulers than we do if Suetonius had not recorded that the Divine Augustus wore a woollen vest next his skin in winter. William of Malmesbury might not have told us that Henry I had a hairy chest and snored.

The *Lives of the Caesars* ran parallel to another type of biography, the eulogy or panegyric. This type, which derived from the funeral oration, was a rhetorical exercise. The eulogist praised the deceased according to rules: he exalted him by dwelling on his noble ancestors and then proceeded on traditional lines. If he were a self-made man, he had raised himself up by his own virtuous efforts. The drawback of both types was that they separated history from biography. No author would have thought of composing a *Life and Times* of his subject: that would have meant mixing up two separate genres.

Valerius Maximus provided history in the form of anecdotes or examples. His *Memorable Deeds and Sayings* (written soon after AD 40) is divided into sections which deal with various kinds of virtues and vices, such as piety and respect for the gods, and the opposite – irreligious behaviour. He subdivided each section into Roman and foreign examples. He hoped to equip the orator with a story for every occasion. This is 'packaged' history. You dip into the collection as though it were a chocolate box. Maximus strengthened the tendency to see history as assorted moral lessons (*exempla*). On the credit side, *Memorable Deeds and Sayings* spread knowledge of both important and trivial episodes in ancient history, and it served as a reference book for encyclopaedists. It became popular, too, with homilists and preachers from the twelfth century onwards. Medieval *exempla* collections were made. How far Maximus inspired them is not known; but he had set an admired precedent.

A good medieval library possessed more books on ancient history than I have mentioned here. I have kept to the main rules and models which came down to historiographers.

The Roman legacy ended with the *Etymologies* of St Isidore, bishop of Seville (d. 636). He produced the standard encyclopaedia of the Middle Ages. A scholar would normally have it to hand and look up the subjects as he needed them. The *Etymologies* come into this chapter, although Isidore was a bishop, because he compiled them from all the scraps of ancient lore available to him in Visigothic Spain in the early seventh century. Much of this information derived from late antique textbooks and reference books which disappeared during the Arab invasions. Where Isidore's sources can be traced to surviving books, he is seen up-ending all kinds of miscellaneous bits of information; but the material passed through his mind; he interpreted it in his own way.

The article on 'History' has a familiar sound with Isidorian overtones. Predictably, history is seen as a subsection of grammar, which itself is part of rhetoric. Grammar Isidore defines as 'the art of writing', and history as 'a written narrative of a certain kind'. He distinguishes history from fable and myth: fable expresses truth by means of fiction, as in Aesop's *Fables*, where animals talk and act like human beings, while poetic myth expresses truth by means of fictions about the gods (a current interpretation of myth as signifying cosmic or moral truths). History differs from these kinds of narrative in being true in itself. It is 'the narration of deeds done, by means of which the past is made known', and derives from the Greek verb 'to see' or 'to know' (a modern dictionary adds 'by enquiry', an important addition to Isidore's derivation). Isidore draws the stark conclusion: since history nar-

10 Opposite: St Isidore of Seville sits at a desk writing his *Etymologies*. The twelfth-century artist portrays him as a young clerk with a tonsure. Isidore was a seventh-century author, who had 'authority'; but his encyclopaedia was ever fresh and constantly referred to in the Middle Ages. The vigour which made him timeless is brought out here. The drawing was executed in England, probably in the late twelfth century. *Cambridge, University Library, MS LI.4.26*

rates what has been seen and known for true, then it must represent an eyewitness account.

None of the ancients would write history unless he had been present and had seen what he narrated; we grasp what we see better than what we gather from hearsay. Things seen are not represented falsely.

It follows that history begins with one's personal experience. The narration of earlier events counts as mere compilation: one just copied one's sources. Isidore did not keep consistently to his narrow view of true history as eyewitness reporting. Elsewhere he classified the various kinds of historical record according to their time span instead: annals record events from year to year; history covers events which have taken place over many years. It was inconsistent of him to recommend Sallust as a historian, when Sallust did not qualify as an eyewitness, for he had not been an exact contemporary of Catiline and Jugurtha. The compiler of an encyclopaedia such as Isidore's does not always reread his articles to check whether he has contradicted himself.

A modern student will object to Isidore's definition of history for two reasons. An eyewitness account need not be historically accurate. 'They saw it happen' is no guarantee of truth, for eyewitnesses give a partial, distorted account of what happened. A second objection will be that the historian of past ages is not just a compiler. He has to discover, select, analyse and interpret his sources. To dismiss him as a mere copyist would be to abolish most historical studies as we know them. The answer is that Isidore oversimplified on his own terms: he did not find any definition of historical research in the notices on historiography which he read in his textbooks. His authorities failed him. Hence he left a confusing legacy to the Middle Ages. No thoughtful medieval scholar could have accepted that an eyewitness account was necessarily true. Canon and civil law procedure required a number of witnesses to attend in court: a witness could be bribed, or prejudiced or mistaken. Medieval historiographers generally trusted the evidence of their own eyes; but they enlarged Isidore's definition to include reports by trustworthy informants. The most scrupulous tell us whether their report is at first hand; if not, they do not vouch for its accuracy. Isidore's most misleading statements were corrected, but he certainly discouraged research on past history by limiting the 'true historian' to contemporary or near contemporary history.

Some positive points emerge from the muddle all the same. The *Etymologies* were a boon as well as a source of confusion to medieval scholars. The bishop of Seville brought a Christian seriousness to bear on the pagan precept that a historian must tell the truth. The divine command 'thou shalt not lie' and the martyr's witness to the true faith inhere in Isidore's definition of history. The medieval scholar could also quote him to justify historiography to those who dismissed it as a mere waste of time. According to Isidore, record-keeping had a practical use: it established chronology by listing the succession of rulers. Dates are useful for other than literary reasons. He also justified historiography from a moral point of view. History has a moral purpose: it teaches us to choose the good and to avoid the bad by supplying us with examples. Pagan history was a necessary supplement to Christian on both counts: the Christian looks to pagan history for both dates and examples. Isidore's list of famous historians begins with Moses, the supposed author of the Pentateuch, and the list goes on to intersperse pagan with biblical and Christian writers.

Looking back at the achievements of medieval historiographers, we may think it just as well that Isidore directed their energies to what we now call 'contemporary history'. He channelled their creative activity into the lines which they were best able to follow. To write the history of the remote past meant copying and compiling; it was not creative. A critical study of the remote past, as distinct from mere compilation of earlier sources, called for tools and equipment which were lacking in the Middle Ages. A few historians had the courage and daring to break out of the Isidorian framework in order to study the remote past. The results did not measure up to the inspiration behind them. The writer's own time and the immediate past offered more scope to his talents and more amenable material. Isidore gave him wise guidance in pointing him away from a task which was beyond his powers.

EVANGELIVM
SECVNMARCVM

3
The Jewish–Christian legacy

Christianity is 'the religion of a book'. A Christian histori-ographer takes the Old and New Testaments as his starting-point. Medieval writings on history make little sense to a reader who does not know his Bible. A medieval writer will normally quote from the Scriptures; he will also refer and allude. Biblical diction and biblical stories colour his tale. He will, however, borrow style and content from the Bible rather than form. His models of form are classical, not bibli-cal. The gulf between Oriental and Western went deep. One could try to be a good Christian; one could not turn oneself into a semite; the classical tradition of writing intervened. A Latin scholar confronted two traditions of historiography. On one side he saw his classical models and rules of composi-tion; on the other he inherited a new time scale, a new framework and a new view of the supernatural. The two legacies amalgamated.

Let us begin with the supernatural in the biblical tradition. The reader of Roman historians would have met it before. They recorded divine intervention in human affairs in the form of omens and marvels. Even such apparent rationalists as Caesar and Sallust mentioned religious beliefs and prac-tices as part of their stories. Modern classical scholarship has uncovered a substratum of folklore and magic in upper-class Latin culture; no one has doubted its persistence among the people. In Christian history the supernatural did not merely impinge on the story; it dominated. The divine element was definite and concrete. God was the creator of the world and the author of its history; he revealed himself in the Scrip-tures. The actors in Scripture were historical characters. The patriarchs and prophets, the Son of God and his Mother and the apostles had all lived on earth. They were not mythical, like the pagan gods and goddesses; their miracles authenticated their teaching; God willed it to be so. The supernatural element increased in the record of post-biblical history. Angels and devils joined the *dramatis personae*. Saints descended from heaven to warn and guide the living and to

11 Opposite: one of the four Gospels, displayed on an altar. A detail from the fifth-century mosaics on the cupola of the Baptistery of the Orthodox at Ravenna. The whole scheme of the dome illustrates the place of the Bible in the Church.

avenge their wrongs. The content of history gained a new dimension. It included heaven and hell.

The new time scale supplied a new framework. Classical authors had held varying views of time. Some imagined it as cyclical: time moved in cycles, variously calculated as the 'great year'. Everything which had happened once would happen again as the 'great year' recurred. The more common view of time in the ancient world was that it moved from past to present towards an indefinitely long future. The Christian view of time differed from both, in that the Christian gave time a beginning and an end. Time existed only between the Creation and the Last Things. Time began with Creation, as recorded by Moses in the first chapters of Genesis. It proceeded through the Old and New Testaments up to the present. It would end with Christ's second coming and Doomsday. Then time and history would give way to eternity. History, seen through Christian eyes, becomes the history of man's salvation in time.

The Bible presented history as it unrolled itself between two definite moments. It was gloriously compact. The Christian reader of any period could marvel at God's perfect plan, embracing past, present and future, although one mortal life covered but a tiny fraction of total history. God's word as set down in Scripture enables us to transcend past and present alike and to foresee their consummation on the last day. St Bonaventure, a Franciscan professor at Paris, found a poetic simile to express this traditionally Christian view of history. He puts it into the prologue to his *Breviloquium*, a compendium of theology, written in 1257. God has ordered his narrative so that it resembles 'a beautiful song', where all things flowing from his Providence can be seen:

No reader can appreciate the beauty of a song unless he looks at all the verses. In the same way, no man can appreciate the beauty of universal order and governance unless he sees it as a whole. No man lives long enough to witness all history with his own eyes; nor can he foresee the future for himself. So the Holy Spirit provides him with the book of Holy Writ, whose length tallies with the course of universal governance, whole and entire.

God opens and shuts the book; but he lets us 'look at the end' to see what will happen on the final page. Divine history is not published as a serial 'to be continued in our next number'. We have it all between two covers; only the span between our present and the end remains hidden, unless God tells us something of it by special revelation. The prophet may foresee what is dark to the historian.

A book needs chapter division to make it readable. The Church Fathers scrutinized the Bible to discover what God had intended by way of chapters in his history of salvation. They invented new periods to serve as chapters, each one marking a stage in the fulfilment of God's plan. Periodization had to include both profane and sacred history; they could not be separated, since both belonged to the workings of divine Providence. It is well to remember that we still periodize history, even when we approach it from a secular point of view. All such divisions have drawbacks; they tend to be artificial and distorting. We use them for the simple reason that no one as yet has discovered any other way to tackle the study and teaching of history. The worst feature of periodization is that it sticks like a well-gummed label. A division of history which reflects the ideas and concerns of one generation imposes its pattern long after it has lost its usefulness. All teachers of history have to struggle with the incubus – 'the Middle Ages closed down on the field of Bosworth in 1485'; 'modern history begins in England with the Tudors'. The ghost of this out-of-date chapter division still haunts us.

Periodization can sometimes act as a stimulant. The Marxist division of history into periods corresponding to the mode of production has led to intensive research and discussion. Fruitful criticism of this kind was inhibited in the Middle Ages by respect for authority. The saints had handed down a set of chapter divisions to be used by readers of God's history book. A medieval scholar would have thought it rash and blasphemous to tamper with tradition. It would have amounted to rewriting the holy page. If he dissented, as some did, he would fiddle with detail or suppress what struck him as untrue, instead of suggesting an alternative. Hence medieval historians inherited a periodization which had been invented in late antiquity and which corresponded to an early Christian outlook on history.

One kind of time scheme was religious in character. St Augustine, the 'chief doctor of the Latin Church', sponsored it with all the weight of his authority. Augustine divided world history into six ages. These represented the six ages of man, as he passes from infancy to senility. God wrote them into history from the very beginning: the six days of Creation, as told in the first chapters of Genesis, signified

12 Opposite: some of the most important events in the history of salvation are painted in roundels set into the initial letter of the opening word of Genesis in the Winchester Bible. Starting at the top, God creates Eve from the rib of Adam; Noah's ark floats on the waters of the Flood; Abraham prepares to sacrifice his son Isaac at God's command; God appears to Moses in the burning bush; John the Baptist baptizes Christ; the Christ Child lies in the manger above Mary and Joseph; finally we see the Last Judgment. All four of the first scenes presage the coming of Christ and his founding of the Christian Church. The manuscript was produced in England about 1160–70. *Winchester Cathedral Library*

both the six ages of man and the six ages of the world. God's rest on the seventh day signified that the world would end in the seventh age, which would mark the transition from time to eternity.

Augustine plotted out the course of his six ages as follows: the period from Adam to Noah represented infancy, Noah to Abraham childhood, Abraham to David youth, David to the Babylonian Captivity of the Jews manhood, Babylonian Captivity to St John the Baptist middle age; the period between the first and the second coming of Christ represented senility: it was the old age of the world. In addition, Augustine subdivided the ages, so as to link each one with its successor. Changing his metaphor, he resorted to the analogy of day and night. Each age had its morning, noon and evening within its span. The night of one age gave way to the morning of the age which followed.

The day and night scheme explains what looks puzzling about Augustine's periodization at first sight: he presented the Christian era as the age of senility, bearing all the signs of sickness associated with growing old. But in terms of day and night, it had its splendour, like the other ages. The sixth age dawned with the Baptist; the sun rose in Christ's Incarnation; the spread of Christianity coincided with midday. Augustine, living in the troubled times of the late fourth and early fifth centuries, supposed that evening would close in soon. The sixth age would give way to the seventh, when time would end. Expectation of the Last Things as due 'at any moment now' tempted Christians to look for signs of the second coming in current events. But Augustine gave them no licence to do so. He condemned speculation on the precise date of Doomsday: we must wait in readiness for the time which God has decided upon without making rash guesses.

The concept of the six ages saddled medieval historiographers with a gloomy picture of their times. Augustine taught that they were living in the old age of the world: noon had passed into evening and night drew nigh. Yet the world lingered on like some aged invalid; there is no cure for senility, however prolonged it may be. Augustine's time scheme discouraged optimism. Progress was ruled out. The individual Christian could grow in virtue by God's grace and merit salvation. There was no hope that mankind would ever improve in the mass.

Such is the resilience of human nature that the prospect of inexorable decline into death did not daunt medieval histor-

13 Opposite: St Augustine's six ages of the world are shown in a circle. They begin with the expulsion of Adam and Eve from the garden of Eden (left, above) and continue anti-clockwise to the Christian era, represented at the top by the Virgin and Child and a priest celebrating Mass. The traditional number of years for the duration of each age is written in the outer circle. An angel with outstretched arms in the centre announces the coming of the seventh age. Then time will end. This picture illustrates a prose translation in Catalan of a Provençal verse encyclopaedia composed in 1288–92. The manuscript was produced in Catalonia in the last quarter of the fourteenth century. The six ages has a long life in historical tradition. *London, British Museum, MS Yates Thompson 31, f.76r*

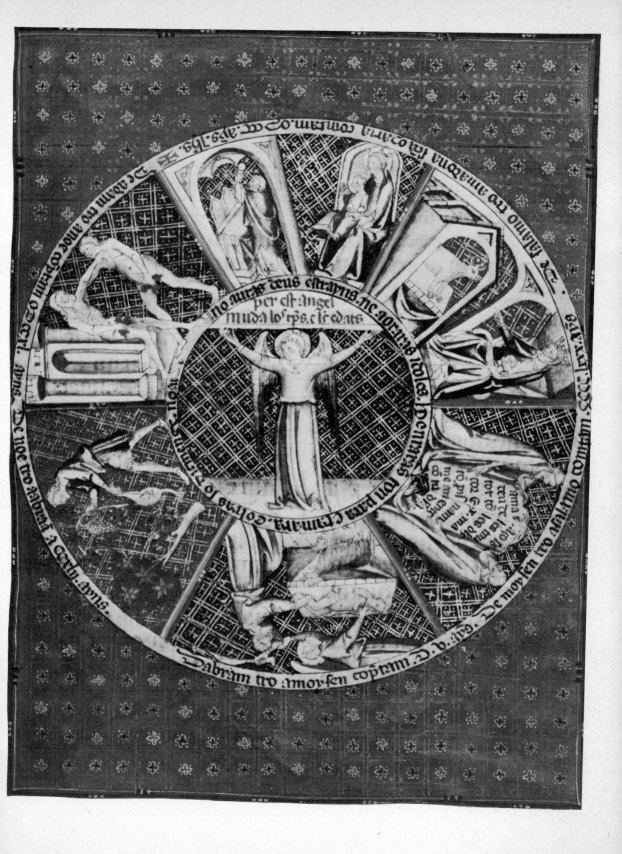

ians nearly so much as one might have expected. Life tasted
good to some of them. Events, however sad and shocking,
had absorbing interest for their recorders. One could not be
indifferent to what was happening in the period before the
lights would be turned off and the stage set for Doomsday.
Many writers, as we shall see, conveniently forgot or ignored
the sadness of their place in a time scheme which they
accepted without question. The idea of the sixth age affixed
itself so firmly and yet sat so lightly on medieval historiography for the very reason that it could not be tested or dis-
proved. A religious theory generally defies the test of fact.
The second time scheme inherited by medieval scholars was
more vulnerable and hence more provocative.

This time scheme is called 'politico-religious'. It originated
in the 'inter-testamentary period', that is the period between
the last of the Old Testament books and the first of the New
Testament. This period saw the desperate struggle of the
Jewish people to defend their religion and preserve their
national identity against their oppressors. Jewish writers tried
to comfort their people and to wring hope out of despair. A
natural way to stiffen resistance was to promise success to
come: the Jews would be rescued by divine intervention in
history. The writers conveyed their promise in a genre known
as the 'apocalypse'.

An apocalypse takes the form of a vision or dream. Its purpose is to prophesy the final triumph of the persecuted people
so as to console them in their misery. The seer, who records
the vision, writes under some well-known name, so as to
make it more noteworthy; he keeps his own name secret.
The most famous apocalypse among Christians passed into
the Old Testament canon under the name of Daniel, the hero
of the story of the lions' den. The writer of this apocalypse
made Daniel live in the period of the Babylonian Captivity
in the reign of 'Darius the Mede'. Darius is a fictitious
character, with no place in history. He stands for a type of
gentile ruler over Jews. Daniel had a vision: he saw three
beasts rise up from the sea, a lion, a bear and a leopard with
four heads. Then a fourth beast, strongest and most terrible
of all, came to chew up the three beasts with its iron teeth and
trample them down with its iron claws. The fourth beast had
ten horns. An eleventh horn, smaller than the ten, sprouted up
among them and mastered them. Lastly Daniel saw the
Ancient of Days, seated on his throne. He ordered that the
fourth beast should be destroyed by burning (Dan. 7).

henr̄ vi · magn̄ Romanoꝝ Impator

Virtutes

fortitudo   Virtutes   Iusticia

fortuna rogat uirtutes
eꞇ ꞇ gꞖoꞯcio eaꝝ ꞅeꞇ re
pullam pafa eſt
deſcende minaꞇꞯꞬ

Roza fortu
ne

Tancred'

The writer, whoever he was, probably meant his four beasts to signify the four world monarchies of which he knew: those of the Babylonians, the Medes, the Persians and the Macedonians. God would destroy the last surviving monarchy and would free His chosen people. When the Romans conquered the Greeks and set up a new world monarchy, the scope of Daniel's vision had to be stretched to include the Romans. The fourth beast now signified the Roman empire. Interpreters of the vision managed to keep the number four by joining the Medes and Persians together as 'the monarchy of the Medes and Persians'. Another passage in the book of Daniel lent itself to the same interpretation. King Nebuchadnezzar dreamed that he saw a statue which had a head of gold, breast and arms of silver, belly and thighs of brass, legs of iron and feet of iron mixed with clay. The statue was destroyed and its metals were scattered to the winds like chaff. This too signified the four world monarchies and the destruction of the last one as a prelude to the day of glory for Israel.

The theme of four world monarchies, which would rise in succession, passed into Christian historiography and supplemented the six ages as a chapter division of universal history. The destruction of the statue and of the fourth beast of the prophecy would herald the coming of Antichrist, signified by the eleventh horn on the head of the beast.

Antichrist and Daniel's ten-headed monster increased their prestige by making an appearance in the Christian Apocalypse. Medieval Latin scholars identified 'John', the author of the Book of Revelation, with St John the Evangelist and the writer of the Epistles of St John. A thirteenth-century English illuminator of Revelation brought out the identification strikingly when he set this last book of the Bible into a picture cycle showing the life and miracles of St John. We see the apostle suffering torture and exile at the hands of the emperor Domitian. He writes his book in exile on the isle of Patmos at an angel's command. Then his book unrolls itself in pictures. Finally, after the last scene of Revelation, the murder of Domitian frees him to return to continue his work of preaching the Gospel and destroying idols. The legendary setting expresses concretely the current belief that Revelation offered an authoritative version of what would happen at the end of time, vouched for in person by the Beloved Disciple.

The theme of Revelation corresponds to that of Jewish apocalyptic, here applied to Christians. John foretells in poetic

Colour plate II
THE WHEEL OF FORTUNE
(see pp. 46–7)
The theme of Fortune's Wheel is knit into the history of the emperor Henry VI (1190–97) in this illustration from the book which the poet Peter of Eboli wrote in his honour. The *Liber ad honorem Augusti* celebrates Henry's conquest of Sicily from the usurper Tancred in 1195. Henry sits crowned holding his orb and sceptre, surrounded by the Virtues, personified. They compete to offer gifts, which the emperor has deserved. Below them we see Fortune's Wheel. Tancred is shown glorying in his luck at the top and then lying at the bottom when Fortune has cast him down. His evil deeds are recorded. He has got what he deserved. Fortune in this context is supposed to reward merit and punish pride and cruelty. She can therefore be enlisted to flatter a ruler. Peter's book is meant as a eulogy. *Bern, Burgerbibliothek, Cod. 120, f.146r*

lucus leonum
ubi daniel missus sua accubba
cuc postcauri sili
ptuus diuus

14, 15 Illustrations from a famous commentary on the book of Revelation by Beatus, a Spanish monk who died in 798. This manuscript from the monastery of S. Domingo de Silos in Castile was finished in 1109. Above: Daniel in the lions' den. Opposite: the vision of the four beasts. The Ancient of Days sits on his throne, whence a stream of fire proceeds. The beasts prance below him. In clockwise order from the upper left, they are the lion with eagle's wings, the four-headed leopard, the bear, and the beast whose eleventh horn (shown with a human head) masters the others. The beasts were interpreted as the four world monarchies (see also ill. 19). *London, British Museum, MS Add. 11695, f. 232r and 240r*

imagery the disasters which God will inflict on his people by means of floods, earthquakes, plagues and wicked rulers. The latter signify persecutors of the Church in general and Roman emperors in particular. Christians must take courage: the triumph of righteousness is at hand. Antichrist embodies the forces of evil in this cosmic struggle. The idea of Antichrist went back to certain Old Testament prophecies and to Jewish apocalypses, though the early Christians first gave him his name. Sometimes he took the shape of a persecuting ruler; sometimes he appeared as a beast or dragon, unleashed upon earth. He wins victories, but finally falls to the spears of the good angels.

John took over the fourth beast of Daniel's vision and presented it as an agent and forerunner of Antichrist. Like Daniel, he sees a beast rising from the sea, having ten horns on its head and upon the horns ten diadems (10:1). The ten horns still signify ten kings, who will fight for Antichrist against the righteous when the end draws near.

The fourth beast of Daniel's vision and of Revelation

36

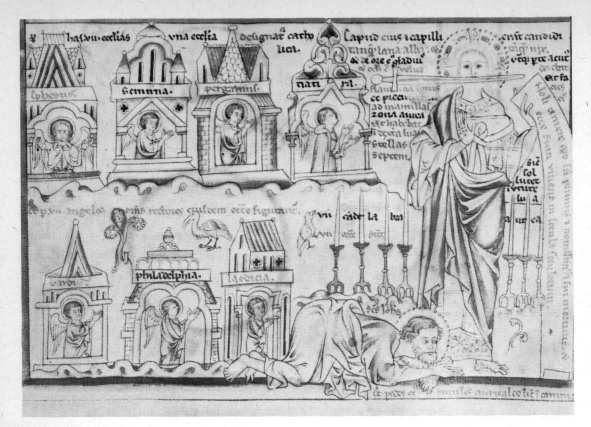

16 The Christian Apocalypse. St John falls at the feet of the Son of Man, who has a 'sharp two-edged sword' in his mouth. The seven churches of Asia to which St John is to send his message and the seven candlesticks of his vision appear at the sides of the picture (Rev. 1:9–17). From a mid-thirteenth-century English manuscript of the school of St Alban's. *Oxford, Bodleian Library, MS Auct. D.4.17, f.3r*

posed many problems. It proved to be a hardy, long-lived creature. The dream statue also persisted in standing upright, in spite of its clay-mixed feet. The beast had recurrent spells of sickness, and the statue tottered at intervals; but they failed to disappear. They survived both in fact and in theory. The division of world history into periods corresponding to the sway of four world monarchies established itself so firmly that it was still taken seriously as late as the sixteenth century. The French scholar Jean Bodin thought himself original and daring when he scrapped the idea of the four-monarchy periodization in his *Method of History* (1566).

The Jewish legacy supplied a model as well as a set of periods. The Jewish author Flavius Josephus wrote his *Antiquities of the Jews* and *The Jewish War* in the late first century A D. His books were translated from Greek into Latin; 'the Latin Josephus' became a 'must' for medieval libraries. Medieval scholars used the *Antiquities* to supplement their Old Testament. *The Jewish War* represented a monograph of the familiar classical type. It went down to the Roman conquest of Jerusalem and the dispersion of Palestinian Jewry.

Josephus was not apocalyptic in outlook – he acquiesced in Roman rule when he could see no alternative – but his book contains vivid battle scenes and a horrifying account of the siege of Jerusalem. Medieval writers found him quotable when they wanted to describe battles and sieges.

The first Christian model of historiography on a large scale came from Eusebius, bishop of Caesarea. He finished his *Ecclesiastical History* in about 325; it was made available in a Latin paraphrase soon afterwards. Eusebius invented a new kind of historiography. No Christian before him had written the history of the Church after the end of the New Testament period. No Christian before him had harnessed universal history to polemic against the pagans. The *Ecclesiastical History* was cosmic in scope. Eusebius set himself to tell the story of divine Providence. God used the Jews directly and the gentiles indirectly for the purpose of man's salvation. Augustus Caesar brought peace to his subjects; hence he prepared them for the spread of the Gospel. The conversion of the emperor Constantine led to the recognition of Christianity as a state religion.

17 The coming of Antichrist as foretold by St John. He slaughters the saints, whose bodies lie unburied, while his servants demolish the holy city. (Rev. 11:2–9). From a manuscript of Beatus' commentary on the Apocalypse (see ills. 14, 15), made at the abbey of St Sever in Gascony in the mid-eleventh century. *Paris, Bibliothèque Nationale, MS lat. 8878, f.155r*

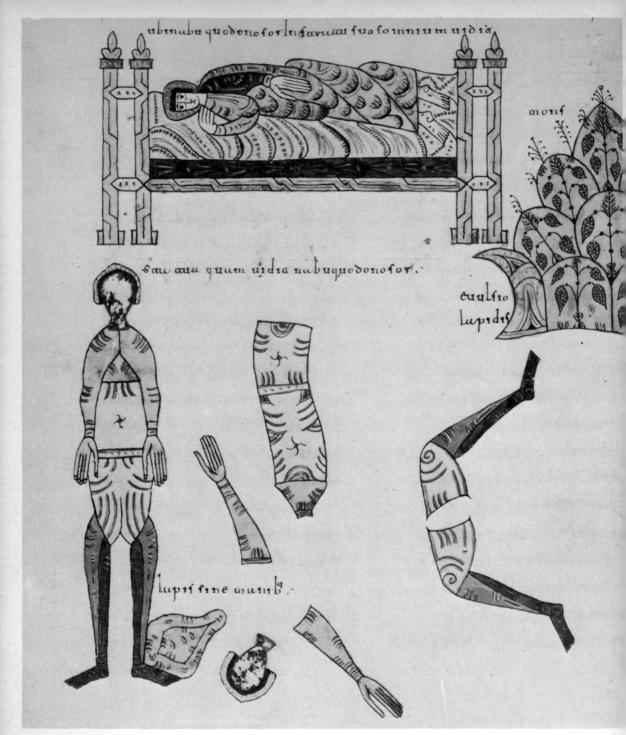

ubinabu quodonofor infarual fuo fomnium uidia

morif

fau aui quum uidia nabuquodonofor.

euulfio lapidif

lupif fine manib.

NEBUCHADNEZZAR'S DREAM OF THE STATUE

18, 19 Above: an illustration from the Silos Apocalypse, finished in 1109 (see ills. 14, 15). The statue is shown first whole and then broken into pieces by the stone 'cut from the mountain without hands'. The stone according to Christian interpretation signified Christ, and its destruction of the statue his final victory over the four world monarchies represented by the different parts of the statue's body.

The image lived on into the seventeenth century. Opposite: a broadsheet published at Augsburg in 1623. The statue is about to be struck by stone. The four beasts (see ill. 15) stand in the background. The eleventh horn of the fourth beast here signifies the power of the Turkish invaders. The prophecy has been brought up to date. *London, British Museum (both; above, MS Add.11695, f.224v)*

Eusebius underlined the all-embracing scope of his *Ecclesiastical History* by drawing up chronological tables to connect biblical-Christian with pagan history. His Christian readers learned from his book that true history must be universal. It was permissible to write a historical monograph; but the historiographer who aimed at something wider must comprehend the history of the whole world. Jewish, gentile and Christian history must be included, since God embraced all three in his plan. Universality became the ideal of Latin historiographers. Eusebius' notion of universality had narrow limits. His world was that of a Greek bishop of the early fourth century. It centred on the Mediterranean and shaded off to darkness outside the imperial boundaries. Medieval historians had to enlarge the area they surveyed, to correspond with the growth of the Church. The focus of history shifted, too, when the imperial provinces of North Africa and Spain fell to the Muslim invaders. The Mediterranean ceased to be the Roman *mare nostrum*, as it had been for Eusebius. Nevertheless, his limited concept of universality had a restrictive effect on medieval writers. They kept his concept in mind and enlarged or shifted their limits only when they could not avoid doing so.

The first attempt at total coverage of world history was not made by a Christian. The Persian scholar Rashēd al Din (d. 1318) compiled a history of the whole world, in so far as it was known to him. He enjoyed the patronage of a Mogul or Mongol emperor, who gave him facilities for collecting information. Rashēd's *History* includes data on places as far apart as Ireland and China. Latin efforts at universal history have a parish-pump appearance in comparison. Still the *Ecclesiastical History* corrected any tendency to mere localism.

Eusebian history was tougher and duller than the classical pagan kind. The rhetorical arguments and techniques which Latin historians used to persuade their readers to fall in with their views did not suit the bishop of Caesarea. He wanted to convince pagans as well as Christians of the truth of his story. He had an up-hill task. The victory of Christianity over pagan cults had put non-Christian intellectuals on the alert: they engaged Christians in a lively dialogue. Eusebius looked for hard proof to confute the pagans. Record evidence filled the bill: he inserted copies of documents issued by the imperial government to accredit his story of persecution followed by toleration. Copies of decrees issued by Church councils and lists of bishops supplied proof for his account of

20 Chronological tables from Eusebius in the Latin translation, showing the dates of Athenian, Latin and Egyptian rulers in parallel columns. From an Italian manuscript of the fifth century. *Oxford, Bodleian Library, MS Auct. T.2.26, f.46r*

ecclesiastical history. He kept it up when he reached a period whose events he could record as an eyewitness. Now, as well as documents, we find references to his own experience. Eusebius describes persons whom he met, places which he visited and buildings which he had seen.

To insert documents meant breaking the rules of rhetorical composition. Suetonius offered a precedent; but he was writing in a less rhetorical genre than Sallust or Livy had chosen. Eusebius' departure from the classical tradition comes out clearly in one particular speech which he includes in his *History*. It is no fake speech, invented as a rhetorical flourish. Eusebius sets down a real sermon, which he preached himself on a solemn occasion, celebrating the rebuilding of the church at Tyre after public Christian worship had been authorized. His sermon belonged to the historical record. The inclusion of documentary evidence in the *Ecclesiastical History* licensed medieval writers to do the same. Following Eusebius, they would copy charters, privileges, papal bulls, letters, decrees and sermons into their histories and chronicles. The modern historian should feel grateful to the fourth-century bishop for setting the standard. Many original documents have been lost, and we rely on copies preserved by medieval historiographers.

The gravest limitation of Eusebian history appears in its title. It is a history of the Church. Secular history has its place only as a framework for ecclesiastical. A medieval historian who wanted to write about politics and battles got no help from Eusebius. Classical models still remained as the only guides to the composition of secular history. There were two

21 Orosius presents his *History Against the Pagans* to St Augustine, bishop of Hippo. The figures are fitted into an initial E in a twelfth-century copy of the *History*. *London, British Museum, MS Burney 216, f.88v*

22 A marginal drawing in the same manuscript illustrates Orosius' account of the first Roman war against Pirrhus. An elephant carries a cart full of soldiers. *London, British Museum, MS Burney 216, f.33r*

possible answers to the problem: one could try to keep secular and ecclesiastical history distinct and write either one or the other, or one could mix two genres. The first solution became ever more difficult to manage, as the Church increased in importance. Medieval historians had no alternative but to write secular and ecclesiastical history concurrently, though the two genres made uneasy bed-fellows.

St Augustine handed down a model as well as a time scheme to later historians. That too was religious. Two historical themes run through his *City of God*. In one, Augustine was arguing against the pagans' objection to Christianity: the Christian God had failed to protect the citizens of the Roman Empire against the barbarian invaders. Augustine answered that Christianity was not to blame for the fall of Rome. Pagan history, he pointed out, recorded both foreign and civil wars, famines and disasters of all kinds. If anything, the miseries of life had been worse in the pagan era than they were in the Christian. His second theme was that mankind throughout the six ages of the world had formed two cities. The city of God confronted the city of the wicked. Abel, the just man, and Cain, his murderer, were the prototypes. The two brothers signified the inhabitants of the two cities for all time. They intermingled on earth, but they would be separated at the Last Judgment. Then the city of God would unite the saved among the quick and the dead; the city of darkness would unite the damned.

Augustine's book represents a vision of history, not a blueprint for historiography. His conception of the two cities is elusive because he never identified the city of God with the visible Church: many professing Christians belonged to the city of darkness. His *City of God*, moreover, was too long and rambling to share the immense popularity of his other works in the Middle Ages. It influenced medieval historians through the distorting medium of Augustine's disciple Orosius.

The *History Against the Pagans* supplied the blueprint for historiography which was missing in the *City of God*. Orosius, a Spanish priest and admirer of St Augustine, undertook to embody his master's ideas in a universal history. His book, presented to Augustine in 417, gives a coarsened version of Augustine's thought, and was popular for that reason. The first theme of the *City of God* lent itself to colourful treatment. Orosius painted a lurid picture of history as a record of the crimes and follies of mankind. Both crimes and follies, mainly committed by rulers, resulted in bloody wars. The historian mounts upon a tower and looks down from his vantage-point at the carnage spread before his eyes. To do Orosius justice, the ancient histories which he read nearly all had 'war' in their titles.

The most original part of his work was his time scheme of the four monarchies. The fourth beast of Daniel's vision represented the Roman empire; but Orosius tamed it. He thought that the empire offered the only shield against the barbarians and hoped that it would last long enough to contain their invasions. Iron teeth and claws have much to commend them, when they bite and trample down one's enemies. Orosius differed from Augustine in this warmth towards the empire. His master realized that the disappearance of Rome as a world power need not mean the end of the world; other states might replace the empire; small states might prove to be less rapacious, because they were less powerful. A careful reading of the *City of God* might have prevented medieval scholars from swallowing Orosius whole. As it was, the *History Against the Pagans* transmitted the idea that the fall of the Roman empire would usher in Antichrist. The ten horns on the head of the fourth beast of Daniel's vision signified ten kings who would divide the empire among themselves. Antichrist would come and master them, as the eleventh horn mastered the ten. His coming would bring those troubles which St John foretold in his Revelation as due to afflict the world before the second advent of Christ.

According to Orosius, his own time fell within the period of the fourth monarchy. The Roman empire was still undivided. Its division would presage Doomsday. The author was so cocksure about the meaning of history that he has been accused of 'playing God to his characters'. This further endeared him to readers who wanted to be told what to think. The *History Against the Pagans* had the merit of being comprehensive and comprehensible. It was one of the most widely read books of the Middle Ages.

Orosius wrote history as a tale of woe, and his imitators followed suit. A ninth-century bishop, Freculph of Lisieux, warns readers of his chronicle:

Almost all writers on history, especially the Greeks and Romans, begin their story with Nimrod, son of Baal, king of many peoples. Their aim is to describe the fortunes of war, the ruin of kings and the miseries of their subjects, so as to teach us that the wars of kings serve only to do them harm.

23 A marginal drawing in the same manuscript of Orosius' *History Against the Pagans* as the two details opposite shows a monster prodigy portending disaster: a child is born with two heads and a double set of limbs. *London, British Museum, MS Burney 216, f.41r*

45

Wars are cruel and futile; but rulers, being fools or criminals, never stop fighting. This is the Orosian point of view. At least, however, Orosius made history seem worth recording. His *History Against the Pagans* had an influence for good inasmuch as it reinforced Eusebius by presenting history as universal. Orosius also taught his readers that geography belonged to history. Sallust and Caesar showed the importance of geography in their monographs; Orosius introduced it on a world-wide scale (in so far as he dealt with 'the world'). He began by giving a geographical survey of the three continents known to him, Europe, Asia and Africa.

King Alfred of Wessex (d. 899) translated Orosius' *History* into English as part of his programme for educating his people. It was one of the basic texts which he thought necessary for their instruction. Since Orosius' geography centred on the Mediterranean, Alfred supplemented it by inserting data on the North Sea and Baltic areas, supplied by a sea captain. The king had taken Orosius' point that geography is a background to history.

Alfred also translated Boethius' *Consolation of Philosophy*, as another indispensable text. Boethius brings us to the last of those key concepts which medieval historians inherited from late antiquity. The *Consolation of Philosophy* is not a history book, but historians took from it the theme of Fortune's Wheel. Boethius wrote as a victim of Fortune. He had served the Arian king of Italy, Theodoric, and had had a brilliant career as a civil servant. Then Theodoric jailed him, suspecting him of taking part in an anti-Arian plot – for Boethius was a Catholic and a Roman, although he had worked for an Ostrogothic ruler. He died in prison in 524. The setting of his *Consolation* is a dialogue between himself as a prisoner and Philosophy, personified as a lady, who comforts him in his ruin. She explains that Fortune has brought him down and goes on to describe the character of Fortune, also personified as a woman. The fickle goddess turns her wheel, now spoiling and coddling her favourites, now dropping them when it pleases her mood. From rags to riches and vice versa they go. Fortune, like a woman, is 'changeable ever'. Why, asks Philosophy, should Boethius complain of her normal behaviour? The wise man will see success as transitory.

Fortune's Wheel became a cliché without losing its pathos. Boethius took care to present the goddess as an instrument of divine providence. Pride goes before a fall, as God has decreed. But her Wheel suggested a theory of causation

24 The lady Philosophy
wearing an embroidered
gown appears to the
senator Boethius as he sits in
prison behind bars. He is
writing his *Consolation of
Philosophy*. From a manu-
script produced at Regensburg in the first quarter of
the thirteenth century.
*Munich, Bayerische Staats-
bibliothek, MS lat. 2599,
f.106v*

within the Christian framework. Orosius displayed the
sweep of universal history; Boethius inserted a proximate
cause for the rise and fall of dynasties, families and individuals. His Fortune deserved her popularity. The modern
historian does not invoke the picture of a goddess cranking
her wheel; but he still resorts to 'chance' in some cases, where
no other explanation occurs to him. There is an incalculable
element in court faction, which ruined Boethius, and in the
feuds and lawsuits of rival families. Fortune's Wheel makes
concrete the elusive, unpredictable factor in human affairs.

47

Hagiography, the writing of saints' lives and passions (their martyrdom), was a flourishing industry all through the Middle Ages. It lies outside the scope of this book, but the student needs to know what its rules and conventions were. The medieval historian would have read or heard *Lives* of the saints; he would often have composed or rewritten *Lives* himself. Hence the genre would influence him when he wrote his chronicle or history.

The conventions of hagiography took shape as early as the fourth century. A Greek *Life* of the hermit St Antony (d. 356) was read in the West in a Latin translation. Sulpicius Severus wrote his Latin *Life* of St Martin of Tours, a bishop and ascetic, toward 397. Here were two model *Lives*, one for a hermit and one for a bishop. Convention prescribed that the author should dedicate his *Life* to a friend, who had asked or ordered him to write. He then apologized in elegant language for not writing elegantly. The degree of elegance depended on his education. Sulpicius belonged to a literary élite and took pains over his style, so he set a high standard.

The presentation of the saint's life normally followed the rules of ancient rhetorical biography or eulogy. The hero fitted into a set pattern: he was saintly from his infancy, or else he was a sinner who was converted to sanctity. The

25 Above: the Wheel of Fortune described by Boethius. The goddess with bands covering her eyes to indicate blindness sits in the centre. A lion, the royal beast signifying pride, stands on the top wearing a crown. The three men, one of whom is losing his crown, signify the changes of fortune experienced by rulers. From a thirteenth-century French manuscript containing a French trans-lation of the *Consolation*. Vienna, Österreichische Nationalbibliothek, MS 2642, f.11r

26 Right: a more elaborate representation of Fortune's Wheel. Here Fortune sits at the side of the picture, not blind but wilfully malicious, turning the wheel by means of a crank. A king, raised up in glory, sits at the top bearing symbols of wealth and enjoyment. Five men fall and rise on the wheel. Fortune's throne rests upon the earth, to signify that change is part of man's earthly condition. From a facsimile of the twelfth-century book called *Garden of Delights* ascribed to Herrad of Landsberg, now destroyed.

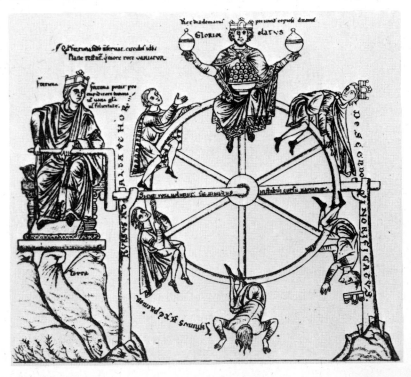

writer had a standard set of miracles to draw upon, such as 'the dream of the pregnant mother' foretelling the fame of her unborn son, a theme which goes back to pagan antiquity. Devils had their stock roles as tempters. Like his predecessor, the ancient eulogist, the medieval writer of a saint's *Life* omitted pettifogging details, such as dates and chronological order. Exceptions are rare. They would have broken the flow of rhetoric; worse still, they would have distracted the reader or hearer from his 'holy reading'. What did dates matter to one's veneration of a holy man?

Sulpicius' literary background led him to introduce a classical note into content as well as style. He opposed St Martin to pagan heroes and sages as the right example for Christians to follow. At the same time, he admired the virtues of good pagans, and knitted them into his story. Biblical precedents are intermixed with pagan. The saint became a hero as 'a soldier of Christ' and also a sage who taught Christian wisdom. Heroines had their parts to play: there were women martyrs, recluses, energetic abbesses.

The saint's *Life* was a semi-historical genre. Its familiarity and its well-established rules marked it out as a neighbour likely to trespass on historiography's domain. The trespass was mainly one way: historians accepted hagiographical traditions of writing more often than hagiographers borrowed from historians. The saint's *Life* offered a tempting model of dateless history.

A question may be asked at this point: why did medieval historiographers need models for their various genres? Why couldn't they write as they thought fit without having to choose a model and mould their story according to its rules? A moment's reflection will show that we still use models, beginning with school essays. New types of history develop slowly. It took a long time for old-fashioned 'political history' to make room for social and economic history, to give one example. The new type edges its way in eventually when new problems oblige us to see the past in a different light and so compel us to accept the unfamiliar. The same process can be seen in the early Middle Ages. New types of historiography were invented to eke out the older types. The classical and Christian models were supplemented by new ones, which could be copied or tailored to fit new needs. Europe after the first wave of barbarian invasions looked so different from the world of late antiquity that its history could no longer be written in the old ways.

4
The barbarian legacy
and the early Middle Ages

27 Brut the Trojan building Stonehenge. From a thirteenth-century French version of the chronicle called the *Brut*. *London, British Museum, MS Egerton 3028, f.30r*

Colour plate III
HISTORY WITHOUT
HISTORICAL
PERSPECTIVE (see pp. 63–4)
Jeremiah, who began to prophesy in 626 BC, foretold that Jerusalem would be conquered as a punishment for the people's sins. His prophecy was fulfilled in the Babylonian capture of the city, in 587 BC. The artist of the Bury Bible – a monk of Bury St Edmunds called Hugh, working about 1135 – shows the prophet holding a scroll with one hand and pointing down to the siege of Jerusalem with the other. The armour, mode of warfare and fortifications belong to the twelfth century. *Cambridge, Corpus Christi College, MS 2, f.245v*

The ancient world had no precedent for the history of a barbarian people. Tacitus' *Germania* is descriptive rather than historical. The Chosen People of the Pentateuch hardly counted as barbarian. But the barbarian invaders of the Roman empire moved triumphantly into historiography just as they founded their successor-states on former imperial territory. They produced four great historians: Jordanes (d. 554?) for the Goths; Gregory, bishop of Tours (d. 593/4), for the Franks; Bede (d. 735) for the English; and Paul the Deacon (d. 799?) for the Lombards. Their histories all survived to a greater or lesser extent. Bede's was the favourite. Later writers quoted, abridged, and embroidered on them.

The unity of history remained unbroken: the invaders, when converted to Christianity, fitted themselves into the pattern of the ancient world. The Romans had set an example in faking origins: Virgil brought Aeneas and his Trojans to Latium to win a kingdom, so as to glorify the early Romans. Jordanes, working on a lost history by Cassiodorus, claimed a mixed classical and biblical origin for the Goths. They descended from the biblical giant Magog and from the Scythians, a people familiar to ancient historians. Gregory of Tours contented himself with the legend that the Merovingians descended from a Frankish princess, who was raped by a sea monster while bathing. Learned invention soon filled the gap. The Franks traced their origin to Noah's son Japhet, who was said to have been the forefather of the Trojans. The Franks' Trojan ancestors wandered abroad as refugees from Troy, and finally settled in Gaul. Bede was too good a scholar to fake pedigrees. He simply told what he knew of the provenance of the Angles, Saxons and Jutes and recorded their claim to descent from the nordic gods. Paul the Deacon, too, admitted a northern origin for the Lombards, although he swallowed the Trojan ancestry of the Franks, 'as our elders have handed it down to us'. In each case the gap between origins and settlement invited fiction, sooner or later: Brut the Trojan was said to have conquered Britain long before the Romans came.

The fashion caught on, so that each town or principality which boasted of any history at all had to have its share in antiquity. The Latin king Turnus founded Tournai; Cracow derives from 'Greek Town', since the Poles were Greek by origin: their forbears had defeated Alexander the Great and then fought their way north to settle in Poland. We may gasp at these fancies; but we ought to remember that barbarian origins remain mysterious to this day. Hypotheses put forward by modern scholars have sometimes been almost as implausible as those of medieval historians.

Had the barbarian invasions brought the Roman empire to an end? That was a serious question. The end of imperial Rome would have broken continuity. More disturbing still, it would herald the coming of Antichrist, as Orosius taught. Barbarian historians had to tackle the problem. Their peoples had effectively destroyed the Roman empire in the West: could they discern continuity all the same, so as to avoid breaking with the classical past and hastening expectations of the end of time? Each of our four barbarian historians found his own answer. One solution was to look East to Byzantium. Rome survived in the East; the Byzantine emperors ruled over all the former territories of the old Roman *imperium* in theory, although in fact the new barbarian kingdoms were independent and had lost any close contact with the successors of the Caesars. Jordanes, Gregory of Tours and Paul the Deacon all took this view, while showing varying degrees of warmth or coolness towards the empire as an institution.

Dissentient voices were heard in Spain, which prepare us to understand Bede's answer to the problem. St Isidore of Seville wrote a history of Gothic Spain, in which he assumed that the Roman empire had disappeared as a world power. He accepted its division into separate kingdoms as a *fait accompli*. Its passing did not strike him as catastrophic: he seems to have thought that division into the ten kingdoms as foreseen by Daniel in his dream might last for an indefinite period. St Isidore's calm in the face of this prospect depended on his idea of the Church as a world power. The Church had replaced the empire; Christianity had spread far beyond the boundaries of ancient Rome. Isidore had witnessed the failure of Justinian's attempt to reconquer the West for Byzantium. He could not hold to the fiction that the Roman empire continued to be one and indivisible. These qualities belonged to the Church.

Colour plates IV, V
UNIVERSAL HISTORY IN CONTEMPORARY DRESS (see pp. 63–5)
Universal history, read as tales of heroes of all ages, is embodied in the Nine Worthies. They form a miscellaneous group, with three representatives from antiquity, three from the Bible, and three from Christendom: Hector, Alexander, Julius Caesar, David, Joshua, Judas Maccabaeus, Arthur, Charlemagne, and the crusading hero Godfrey of Bouillon. They became popular in the late Middle Ages, especially as a theme for pageantry. These wall-paintings in the church at Dronninglund in Denmark show them in fifteenth-century dress. In the detail above, Alexander the Great (seated on an elephant) confronts King Arthur; below, Charlemagne confronts Joshua.

28 The end of the fourth monarchy would herald the coming of Antichrist; hence the urgency of determining when it would end. Here Antichrist is depicted in a terrifying form as a monster riding on the back of the sea beast, Behemoth. From the Encyclopaedia of Lambert of St Omer, finished before 1120 (see also colour plate I). *Ghent, University Library, Liber floridus, f.62r*

A.

Voden gen vectam. q̅g̅ uictam. q̅g̅ Wichtgils. q̅g̅ horsam æhen gest.

c. Voden g̅ Beldei. q̅g̅ Brond. q̅g̅ freodegarū. q̅g̅ freawinū. q̅g̅ Vra gosfrisse. q̅g̅ Esla. q̅g̅ q̅g̅ Cerdic.

g. Woden g̅ freothulge æt. q̅g̅ vaga. q̅g̅ wich dæg. q̅g̅ Vermundum. q̅g̅ offa. q̅g̅ Ongeltheou. q̅ g̅ Comerū. q̅g̅ Iced. q̅g̅ Cnibbā qui g̅ kineswaldū. q̅g̅ Crydā. q̅g̅ Bibbā. q̅g̅ pendam.

f. Voden g̅ Beldei. q̅g̅ Brond. q̅g̅ Benoc. q̅g̅ Aloc. q̅g̅ Ange nuuta. q̅g̅ Inguin. q̅ Etam. q̅g̅ Eopā. q̅g̅ Idam. a q̅ reges Northanhimbrorū ceput originē.

d. genuit Vuelgeat a q̅ ...

Voden g̅ Wegdam. q̅g̅ sigegarum. q̅g̅ sweabdegum. q̅g̅ sigegeat. q̅g̅ seabaldum q̅g̅ seafugel. q̅g̅ Westerfalcne. q̅g̅ Wilgils. q̅g̅ Vscfrea. q̅g̅ yffe. q̅g̅ Ella.

Exfert notata serie generationum eroqua primi anglia generis reges prohibent sub notatur qui æcū æquoto incarnat anno regnauerint p̅ illorū ad puentum inbrittanniam.

Anno ab incarnatione dñi. cccc. xl. yr. anglorū siue saxonum gens in uitata arege Wurtigerno trib: longis nauib: brittanniam aduehit. apud locum q̅ dicitur cypwinesfleot. quasi pprætria pugnatū. re autem uera hanc expugnatū suscepit. Aduenerat aū de trib: germanie. poplis. fortioribus. id est saxonib: anglis. iutis. De iutarum origine sunt Cantuarii & uectu arii. hoc est ea gens que uectam tenet insulam. & ea que usq: hodie in puin cia occidentalium saxonū. iutarum ratio notatur. posita contra insulam uectam. De saxonibus id est ea regione que nunc antiquorū saxonū ...

Bede was even more detached from the empire than Isidore. Byzantium was too remote to interest him. He accepted the six ages of the world, as handed down by tradition, but suppressed the four monarchies as a time scheme. His mind moved along the same lines as Isidore's in that he believed that religious unity transcended political. Britain had once been a province of the Roman empire. Now missionaries from Rome had converted the English and organized the Church in England as a daughter of Rome. English missionaries were converting the heathen Frisians. What did the lapse of the Roman empire matter? We shall see that it did still matter to some historians. The English and Spanish writers had buried the fourth monarchy prematurely.

Another urgent problem faced barbarian historians. Their models tended to separate sacred from secular history: could the history of a barbarian people follow such a division or must the two kinds of history be amalgamated? Barbarian history forbad the separation of its subject-matter into two parts. Conversion to Christianity, whether Catholicism or Arianism was chosen, marked a turning-point in a people's history. It affected their way of life, their institutions and their relations with their neighbours. Jordanes, Gregory of Tours and Paul the Deacon include religious history as an integral part of their stories. Bede made an attempt at separation; he concentrated on the Church, and he called his book *The Ecclesiastical History of the English People*. Secular history comes into it however. There is a larger element of the secular in Bede's *History* than there is in Eusebius'. The fortunes and preferences of English kings bore heavily on the endowment of churches and monasteries and on the careers of churchmen. The mixture of sacred and secular in historiography had come to stay.

A legacy of unresolved tension remained. Barbarian historians handled two sets of values, which clashed with each other. The writer felt proud of his people's heroic past; he loved to record the pagan warlords' splendid deeds. As a churchman, the writer could show that a successful warrior's conversion reflected glory on Christianity. The trouble was that baptism seldom led to the practice of Christian virtues. The historian found it easier to identify himself with his people, and would forgive a ruler's sins against the Church's teaching, provided that his kingdom flourished in his reign. Religion might be carried to excess in a ruler. His people

29 Opposite: the god Woden is represented as the ancestor of Anglo-Saxon kings in a treatise on the succession of kings of the Heptarchy, tracing their descent from Woden. The manuscript is written in an English hand of the early thirteenth century. Woden, shown in the centre of the picture, is conceived in the style of contemporary representations of God and of Christian kings. *Liège, University Library, MS 369 C, f.88v*

30 The beginning of book iv of Bede's *Ecclesiastical History*, from a manuscript written in southern England in the late eighth century. *London, British Museum, MS Cotton Tiberius C.II, f.94r*

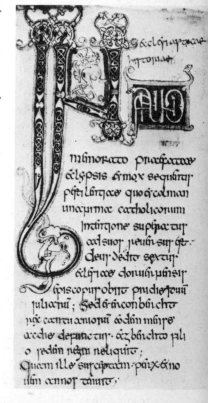

might suffer if he renounced the world in order to enter a monastery or go on a pilgrimage.

To write a saint's *Life* was a less difficult assignment than to record the deeds of a king. The saint could combine wisdom with heroism in a Christian framework; but the saint was often a churchman. Few kings were canonized, and kings made history. We shall see how medieval historiographers wrestled with the problem of writing about Christian kings. Orosius' Olympian view of history held good only for the author of a universal history. To record the history of a people meant taking sides and rejoicing in victories over one's enemies. Then the Old Testament model came to the rescue. A writer could annex the role of the Israelites for his people. Their enemies joined the ranks of the gentiles, who deserved to be destroyed. All too easily, the Christian God became a tribal god, fighting on the historian's side. But particularist passion gave excitement to what would otherwise look like mere minor raids and border skirmishes.

Conditions for study of any kind worsened during the sixth and seventh centuries. The pattern of the early Middle Ages slowly emerges in the barbarian kingdoms. It centres on cathedrals and monasteries. The bishop has responsibility for teaching in his diocese. His main duty is to train his clergy. He may teach in person in his cathedral school. Many cathedrals were built in old provincial capitals of the Roman empire and might inherit a rich library: Verona, Ravenna and Lyons are examples. A conscientious bishop would encourage the copying of texts; private patronage of scribes was needed more than ever, since the public book trade had reached a standstill. Besides the cathedral, the monastery played its part in preserving culture. There were 'city monasteries', such as Fulda, St Gall and Monte Cassino. Abbots regarded their library and *scriptorium* as integral to their little 'state within a state'. Political disorder and travel difficulties did not put an end to intercourse between scholars. Cultural exchanges between the main centres of learning continued throughout Western Christendom.

New types of historiography developed to meet new needs. The most primitive form of medieval historical record was annals. They started within the modest framework of tables for reckoning the date of Easter. This is still a movable feast, but its computation has been standardized; we have only to look in our diaries. It was a question of 'do it yourself' in this early period. The mode of reckoning was stan-

31 Tables for the calculation of Easter with historical matter written into the margin and between the lines. From a German manuscript of the third quarter of the tenth century, from Einsiedeln. *Einsiedeln, Stiftsbibliothek, Cod. 29 (878)*

dardized slowly, as was the custom of counting in years from the beginning of the Christian era, 'BC' and 'AD'. Various modes of reckoning competed, and writers would sometimes use several concurrently. The movable feast of Easter determined the whole course of the Christian year, with its round of festivals and fasting. Hence monastic and minster churches needed tables which would show the date of Easter and ensure that services could be arranged beforehand. Tables were compiled to establish dates over a number of years.

A table inevitably offered blank spaces, which attracted notices of events. The computist, or someone who used his tables, would enter the record of a storm or comet or an occasion of local interest or the death of some great person. The next stage in the process of keeping annals was to have the entries copied out separately from the tables. The annals would then be kept up to date either systematically or by fits and starts. The monks of one abbey would borrow annals from another; they would make their own additions to the original and would continue it as the years passed. Their practice has worried modern scholars: to write history correctly it is necessary to isolate the original set of annals or find the common source drawn upon by the various compilers. The task has been compared to peeling an onion: a medieval set of annals always has another skin underneath. Monastic annals as a genre are uncouth, unclassical (in spite of the name) and generally derivative; but they kept historiography alive in circles where nobody felt like attempting ambitious literary history. Education and motive were lacking.

Another influential piece of record-keeping was the *Liber Pontificalis* or *Pope's Book*. The popes functioned as bishops of Rome as well as heads of the Latin Church. The former capacity is more in evidence in the early stages of their *Book*. Clerks (who in the Middle Ages were clerics as well) in the Lateran writing-office recorded the apostolic succession and added papal biographies. We refer to the *Liber Pontificalis* as a 'book' for convenience; the name is collective rather than singular in this case. It resembles a wood of trees, which thickens in some parts and thins out in others, rather than a single tree-trunk with branches. It has come down to us in a number of different versions. Its compilers in the early Middle Ages were mainly 'backroom boys' who, as papal employees, wrote anonymously. Some biographers had a propaganda purpose, in that they wished to justify papal policies *vis-à-vis* other powers, but their interests were chiefly local. The popes figure as bishops of Rome. The Romans depended on their bishops as wealthy landowners to feed the city in times of famine and to keep it habitable by looking after water supplies and drainage. The popes shouldered their responsibilities; and they also took pride in building and decorating Roman churches. To choose one papal biography as an example: the biographer of Honorius I (625–38) records his gifts and repairs to Roman churches, setting down the exact weight of precious metal spent on each of them. A later addition to Honorius' *Life* states that he installed a mill in a place called 'Trajan's Water' and that he mended the aqueduct there. No reader would guess from the *Life* that Honorius played an active part in organizing the early Church in England. That was too distant to interest his biographer.

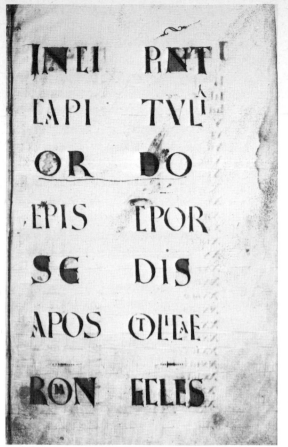
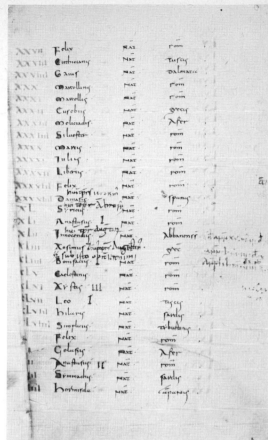

The *Liber Pontificalis* became widely known. Scholars consulted it when business brought them to the papal court. Parts of it were copied and circulated. The papal biographies suggested new ideas to historiographers whose main reading consisted of the *Lives* of saints. The early medieval popes were not saints or martyrs, but ordinary men, dealing with practical problems. Gregory I stands out as exceptional. The *Popes' Book* showed readers that it was worth while to record the doings of churchmen who had no claims to holiness. It served as a model for *Deeds* of bishops and of abbots. Paul the Deacon knew the *Popes' Book* and had it in mind when Charlemagne asked him to write a history of the bishopric of Metz. His *History of Metz* set a pattern for later historiographers. This type of history began with the foundation of the see or abbey (the account was often legendary). The writer copied such sources as he could find and went on to

32, 33 Two pages from a copy of the *Liber Pontificalis* made in the eighth or ninth century, from the abbey of St Remigius at Rheims. Above left: the title page. Above: part of the list of popes, successors of St Peter, with their places of origin. *Leyden, University Library, Cod. Voss. lat. 9.60, f.5r and 6r*

describe more recent happenings. He used the reigns of successive bishops or abbots as his chronological framework. The pattern made it easy for later writers to add to the story and keep it up to date.

The scope of these *Deeds* would vary according to the importance of the bishops or abbots. They might take part in the affairs of Christendom as a whole or they might be stay-at-homes. In the former case we see what world politics looked like to a local observer; in the latter we may hear more about the local town and countryside. These local historiographers bring us closer to social and economic history than do any others. No writer envisaged a history of 'the common people'. Modern scholars depend on documentary evidence rather than on literary sources when they study the history of medieval peasants. But the writer of *Deeds* had occasion to mention countrymen and townsmen, landlords and travellers, because their customs, feuds and risings and their generosity or robbery affected his community. Local history joined the historical monograph as an alternative to universal history or the history of a people. It had its secular counterpart in *Deeds* of princes or histories of a ducal family.

Secular *Deeds* bring us to a third type of centre for scholarship, the princely court. Barbarian rulers listened to tales of their heroic forbears; the interest of these stories was enlarged by what happened after their conversion to Christianity. Bede dedicated his *Ecclesiastical History of the English People* to a Northumbrian king. In France the Mayors of the Palace who replaced the last Merovingians had historians among their courtiers. Under the Frankish court of Charles Martel (d. 741) the weak beginnings of the cultural revival associated with his grandson Charlemagne (d. 814) could be seen. Charlemagne and his advisers worked hard to establish a learned clergy and to remedy the shortage of books and teachers. Their efforts bore fruit in a great output of learned writing, which started in the last years of Charlemagne's reign and continued up to the mid-ninth century. We know now that the 'Carolingian Renaissance' began earlier and took longer to get off the ground than used to be thought.

Cathedrals, abbeys and the imperial court all contributed to the revival. This association meant that upper-class laymen could share in literacy and authorship. Monastic and cathedral schools accepted external pupils. Two ninth-century historiographers, Einhard and Nithard, were both laymen. This gives

a special richness to Carolingian historiography. The reading and writing of Latin became a clerical monopoly as the ninth century passed: laymen lost either the inclination or the leisure to study. At best they figured as hearers or readers; they needed translations from Latin, and they did not write books.

The 'Dark Ages', as we ungratefully call them, added much that was new to the existing stock of genres. A historiographer of the early ninth century had a wider choice than had been available five hundred years earlier. Like an artist, he could go in for wall-painting in the form of universal chronicle or world history, or the history of a people; alternatively, he could choose to paint in miniature in the form of the story of his church or his abbey or of

34 Local monastic history. The monk Purchard kneels to present his verse *Deeds* of his abbot, Witigowo of Reichenau, to the abbot, who stands to the left of the Virgin and Child. The monks look on. At the far left a personification of the island of Reichenau supports the abbey. Purchard wrote about 994–6, adding to his local history an account of the abbot's journey to Rome with Otto III for his imperial coronation. This is a unique manuscript produced near the time of writing. *Karlsruhe, Badische Landesbibliothek, MS Aug. CCV, f.72r*

61

35 An example of mis-information culled from travellers' tales. Adémar of Chabannes, a chronicler of the early eleventh century living near the pilgrim centre of Limoges, illustrated his text by a sketch of the tomb of Charlemagne in the church at Aachen. Adémar got the architectural detail wrong. *Rome, Biblioteca Apostolica Vaticana, MS Vat. lat. 263, f.235r*

biography. A less enterprising writer could limit himself to keeping up the local annals.

The moment has come to mark out the main differences between medieval and modern historians. The most obvious is the medieval notion of time and space. The medieval historian's time enrolled itself between the Creation and Doomsday; it began and it would end; it moved through clearly defined periods. His space was circumscribed by the limits of ancient and biblical history in the past and by the extent of Christendom in the present. There were travellers' tales of outside peoples, but they hardly count as history. Non-Christian peoples normally entered into history only in so far as the Christian historian recorded border warfare or raids or missions to the heathen. Another obvious difference is that the medieval historian had a much smaller stock of tools for investigating the past than we have. He relied upon literary sources and hearsay. An observant author could look at ancient monuments and try to use them as evidence; but he could not bring scientific techniques to bear on what he saw, read or heard.

The main obstacle to our understanding of medieval historiography is absence of perspective. Medieval figurative art is two-dimensional. The artist paints or draws on a flat surface. The student of medieval art learns to accept the flatness as a convention: it does not spoil his appreciation of the picture. In the same way, the student of medieval historiography must learn to do without perspective in historical presentation. A medieval writer could distinguish stages in the history of salvation, but they were religious stages. He did not discern change or development in temporal history. He saw continuity in customs and institutions, where we see diversity. Roman emperors are made to talk and behave like medieval rulers. Alternatively, a writer learned in the Latin classics tended to make medieval rulers talk and behave like the Caesars. The historian did not only look back to the Old and New Testaments for parallels and precedents; he lived in an expanding Bible. The writer of a saint's *Life* felt that he was adding a new page to the Gospel story; the recorder of a warrior's deeds was continuing the tale of ancient and Old Testament heroes. Past and present interlock: ancient precedents imposed themselves on the present; the past resembled the present as the historian saw it. He had no sense of anachronism.

Neither had the medieval artist. Here, too, we find a parallel. The artist did not aim at historical correctness when he designed persons and buildings: he dressed his characters in medieval costume, or else he copied from an earlier model; sometimes he produced a mixture. The artist of the twelfth-century Bury Bible shows Jeremiah in his prophet's uniform of classical drapes, sitting on a cloud. In the lower half of the picture we watch the capture of Jerusalem, which the prophet has foretold. This scene has a twelfth-century

36 The martyrdom of St Lawrence was seen as a continuation of the Gospel story. St Lawrence carries a cross and an open book. He stands beside the gridiron, rolled into the place of his martyrdom on its wheels, on which he was burnt. On the other side stands a cabinet containing the four Gospels which he preached. A fifth-century mosaic in the Mausoleum of Galla Placidia at Ravenna.

setting. Armour, costume and fortification are all depicted in the contemporary idiom. The incident has a living intensity, just because the artist sees it as taking place in the present.

Nowadays the historian thinks it his business to trace and to interpret change. He looks for continuity, too; but he regards it as a thread which runs through the changing pattern of history. Anachronism is his bugbear. Historical novels make painful reading if the characters in them wear the wrong sort of clothes or express sentiments out of keeping with their period. Our way of looking at history as a record of change contrasts with the lack of perspective shown by medieval historians. They may strike us as funny and naïve, but we must try to understand their ideas in the light of medieval conditions. Then we shall see that absence of perspective had its ground in reality.

The medieval view of past ages as all alike was rational, in that essentials had not changed. The ancient past, as it was known to the Middle Ages, had many features in common with medieval society up to the fifteenth century at least.

Production was unmechanized; the bulk of the population worked on the land; literacy was limited to a larger or smaller élite; the supernatural was ever present in one form or another; the New World was unknown. Changes and improvements in agriculture, industry and transport happened slowly in unspectacular ways. Today, the pace forces us to realize that we live in a different world from that of our grandparents' day. Nor is lack of perspective peculiar to the Middle Ages. Beginners often have difficulty in charting a time scheme before the age of discoveries or the industrial revolution. BC and AD are all the same to them. It is a privilege of children who have sophisticated parents and a chance to see historical monuments to grow up with a sense of period. Otherwise it comes gradually, if at all. Medieval men had a past where they could feel at home. We are strangers to ours. The historian has to make an effort to acclimatize himself in the Middle Ages. Then he must pack and start over again if he wants to visit the ancient world. Medieval historiographers travelled light.

38 An example of historical anachronism. Oedipus fights the sphinx. He wears late thirteenth-century armour and emerges from a contemporary castle. The picture illustrates a copy of the *Histoire universelle*, a compilation on world history from the Creation to Julius Caesar, written in French and intended to be read to a lay audience. This manuscript was produced at Acre, the capital of the Latin kingdom in Palestine, about 1285. *London, British Museum, MS Add. 15268, f.77v*

5

Royal biographies
c. 800–c. 1150

Royal biographies have one feature in common: they are propaganda pieces. The writers' purposes and techniques varied, but they all had to find a mould which would contain the unruly facts. The prince had to be presented as his biographer wished to show him to his readers or hearers.

We begin with Einhard, the biographer of Charlemagne. Einhard was a short man in stature, and he wrote a short book. It has a long history; its influence was out of proportion to its size. The author was a layman, in contrast to later biographers. The Carolingian revival of learning put a good education at the disposal of laymen who had connections with the court. Einhard was well read and well equipped to write Charlemagne's *Life*. He had served Charlemagne in the emperor's old age and then passed into the service of Charlemagne's successor, Louis the Pious. Einhard did not start from scratch, since historiography was already a state enterprise; the keeping of royal annals had begun. He was asked to write a *Life* of Charlemagne, and composed it within the years 829–36. A good Isidorian, he excuses himself for being a 'mere compiler' for the early and middle years of his hero, which fell outside the range of his memory. Recent research on the *Life* has shown that he did not shine as a compiler, being careless in handling his sources. When he reached the emperor's old age, however, he could write as an eyewitness.

Einhard might have searched in vain for a Christian model to guide him in writing the life of a secular ruler. The genre of biography familiar to him would have been *Lives* of saints, and these were quite unsuitable. A classical model lay ready to hand in Suetonius' *Lives of the Caesars*. Einhard chose Suetonius as his guide. He wrote what has been called 'the thirteenth *Life* of a Caesar' to add to Suetonius' twelve. The ninth-century biographer imitates his model's structure and style, to the extent of omitting biblical quotations and phrases. No scriptural reminiscences sully the purity of his Latin. It must have cost him an effort to avoid what a

39 Opposite: the Carolingian tradition inspired the three Saxon emperors, Otto I, II, and III. Here an Ottonian emperor sits in majesty, crowned and holding the orb and sceptre. From an ivory situla, executed about 1000, from Aachen. *Aachen, Cathedral Treasury*

40 An idealized portrait of Charlemagne set into the initial of the opening word of Einhard's *Life*, from a manuscript produced in France in the eleventh century. *Paris, Bibliothèque Nationale, MS lat. 5927, p. 280*

classicist would have regarded as contamination. Einhard kept afloat by borrowing items as well as reproducing the style of his Latin original. He picked out details from the various *Lives* where he could adapt them to his account of Charlemagne. Sometimes he had no parallel in any *Life*. The Caesars had been literate, whereas Charlemagne began to learn his letters too late in life to make much progress. Einhard had no scruples about recording this barbarian trait. He was a creative writer as well as an imitator. A convincing portrait of the aged emperor emerges; but alas! Einhard's choice of Suetonius makes his story a riddle to modern historians. He followed his guide in avoiding both comment and value judgment. We can read his silences as we like. We do not know what he thought of Charlemagne's attitude to the Church. He describes the emperor's piety in classical terms, merely adding 'Christian' as an adjective to 'religion'. The question arises: did his love of antiquity motivate him to keep his hero's religion as close to the Caesars' as possible? Or is there more to it? Did Einhard use his model for a more positive end? Did he choose it as a medium to express secular heroic values to the detriment of Christian?

The most important evidence for the second question comes from Einhard's account of Charlemagne's coronation by the pope at Rome on Christmas Day 800. Much has been deduced from it. Einhard gives the initiative to the pope and presents Charlemagne as unwilling to accept the crown. He was taken by surprise, according to Einhard, and said that he would not have gone to church that day, had he known what the pope was planning to do. Perhaps Einhard implies in this statement that Charlemagne would have preferred to take the imperial title without benefit of clergy, thinking it undignified for a great conqueror to be crowned by a churchman. Perhaps he had no use for the imperial title at all. His conquests and his inheritance gave him power and glory enough as king; why pose as emperor? Einhard also tells us that Charlemagne found his new title a hindrance to good relations with the Byzantines, who objected to a Western ruler usurping their role. All we can safely say about Einhard's attitude is that he chose a secular model for his biography and that he did nothing to clericalize Suetonius. Just how secular his values were is a matter of opinion. It is equally difficult to say how far his values reflect those of Charlemagne. We do not know whether Charlemagne confided in his courtier or not.

41 Einhard's love of the antique appears in the reliquary that he gave to the abbey of St Servatius at Maastricht, of which he became lay abbot in 815. This is a seventeenth-century drawing of the base of the reliquary, now lost. It was the first medieval specimen of goldsmith's work decorated with figures. An inscription in antique style set over a Roman triumphal arch records Einhard's donation. Below it a rider tramples on the forces of evil represented by a dragon. Other details represent the four Evangelists, the Annunciation and various Christian themes, all influenced by ancient models. *Paris, Bibliothèque Nationale, MS fr. 10440*

This enigmatic masterpiece influenced later biographers, but its very nature prevented them from copying it slavishly. Einhard's successors were clerks, not laymen. Hence they had a less secular outlook. Their subject-matter differed too. There was no second Charlemagne, and churchmen loomed larger in politics after he died. The break-up of his empire did not lend itself to the kind of admiring detachment which Einhard had found in Suetonius' *Lives of the Caesars*.

The break came immediately. The career of Louis the Pious, Charlemagne's son, called for pity rather than praise and thanksgiving: his troubles and humiliations made sad reading. Thegan, his first biographer, was assistant bishop of Trier and a strong partisan of Louis. He departed from the Suetonian structure in favour of a narrative form, so as to bring out the drama. Far from avoiding biblical language, he wallowed in its expressiveness. The Latin Old Testament offered an unrivalled vocabulary to convey the emotions of wrath and grief, and Thegan exploited it to the full. Instead of keeping himself in the background, as Einhard did, he bursts into exclamations and prayers. Louis' piety appealed to him as a churchman. Thegan dwelt on the emperor's humble attitude to the pope and on his moral strictness. Louis was more puritanical than his father. He never laughed or showed his white teeth in a smile even on feast days, when all around him were enjoying music and mummery. The question why so good a Christian should have suffered calamity led Thegan to broach historical analysis. He picked on a human, political cause. The emperor chose 'evil counsellors', low-born men, who betrayed him. Louis had acted against the principle of hierarchy. Great men were the natural advisers of a ruler.

The contrast between Einhard and Thegan as biographers struck their contemporary, the scholar abbot Walafrid Strabo. He edited Einhard's *Life* and added a preface, praising his learning, character and political astuteness, qualities fit to guarantee his reliability as author. Strabo excuses Thegan for writing less well than Einhard and for showing bias: Thegan had little time to spare from his duties as bishop; his love of justice and partisanship for Louis caused him to exaggerate. In Strabo's eyes, Einhard had produced the more elegant and trustworthy biography.

A younger contemporary of Thegan wrote a second *Life* of Louis the Pious. Thegan had stopped before the emperor's death in 840. The second biographer brought the tale up to date. He wrote anonymously: we know only that he was a clerk and a courtier. Modern historians call him 'The Astronomer', on account of his interest in the stars and planets. His method as a biographer puts him in a halfway-house between Thegan and Einhard. He followed Einhard in quoting less often from Scripture than Thegan. His values were more secular than Thegan's; he plays down the emperor's meekness in greeting the pope. But he was pulled two ways. The Astronomer departed from Einhard's structure in choosing a mainly narrative form for his biography. He sometimes treats himself to a purple patch, which would have offended the purists. The devil, that unclassical figure, slips into his story, stirring up Louis' sons to rebel against their father.

Another early medieval biographer tried to imitate Einhard. Asser, bishop of Sherborne, took the *Life of Charlemagne* as his model when he wrote his *Life of King Alfred* (893).

Asser did his utmost to fit the story of Alfred into Einhard's pattern, but he did not succeed. The influence of saints' *Lives* creeps in, since he wanted to present the English king as a holy man. Einhard's narrative was too dry. Asser wanted more unction and pathos. According to Asser, Alfred, like Charlemagne, learnt to write in his middle age, with the aim of teaching his people in the aftermath of the Danish wars. A biblical comparison gives solemnity to the story of Alfred's endeavours to cope with book learning. Asser likens him to the penitent thief, who was crucified with Jesus and entered late into the joys of paradise. The biographer brings himself into the picture, just as Thegan did. Asser describes how he encouraged the king to read and to collect extracts for his 'commonplace book'. The churchman's patronizing tone when writing of a layman, even of so gifted and pious a layman as Alfred, comes through his story. The result is very different from the *Life of Charlemagne*.

Einhard eluded his imitators, fortunately for the history of biography. A clerk could not write like a layman, nor would he sacrifice drama and excitement by avoiding narrative form and emotional comments on his tale. When he could not copy, he had to invent. The Einhards *manqués* were compelled to be creative.

Our next royal biographer gave up any idea of modelling himself on Einhard. Helgald, monk of Fleury-sur-Loire, wrote a *Life* of the French king, Robert the Pious, soon after Robert's death (1031). Helgald imitated the form of a saint's *Life*, and his book would have been read aloud to a religious community for edification. Robert appears as an ideal Christian king. Humble, kindly and orthodox, he protects churches and people against evildoers. So great was his virtue that he merited to work miracles. Helgald had to do some editing. By calling his *Life* an 'epitome', he covered himself for not telling everything. This allowed him to omit whatever struck him as unsuitable. He left military and political history right out. The early Capetian kings of France kept their heads above water, but only just. King Robert was not a conquering hero. His orthodoxy needed editing too. Helgald does not mention the king's matrimonial troubles and his excommunication by the pope.

Suetonius and Einhard make a sudden and welcome appearance. Helgald turned to them to fill the gap which he noticed in the *Lives* of saints. They suggested a pen portrait. The monk of Fleury had visited the court on business of his

42 A twelfth-century stained glass window in Strasbourg cathedral shows the emperor Conrad II and his son Henry III.

abbey and had met Robert in person. He drew on his memory to write a vivid description of Robert's physique and characteristics. We even hear how the king sat his horse. The portrait stands out as a triumph of observation in a conventional setting.

The empire offered grander stuff to the biographer than the French kingdom in the eleventh century. Its bounds were wider: the German emperor ruled over the duchies of Lorraine, part of Burgundy and Lombardy, while exercising a protectorate over the papacy. The peoples across his eastern border came under his influence in varying degrees. We have a biography of the emperor Conrad II, written by his court chaplain, Wipo, in 1046. Wipo wrote it for the benefit of Conrad's son, Henry III. The biographer intended to restore official imperial historiography, which had lapsed during his lifetime. His *Life of Conrad* would provide Henry III with an account of his father's policies and military campaigns. Wipo further planned to make a record of Henry's deeds for the use of future biographers. As Conrad's chaplain, Wipo could write as an eyewitness; he had good opportunities to observe and to collect data at first hand. Sometimes illness kept him away from court, and in that case he scrupulously tells us so and says that he relies on trustworthy informants.

Like Helgald, Wipo had a religious purpose; but he was more ambitious. Helgald modelled his *Life* of King Robert on a saint's *Life*, throwing in a dash of Einhard to make it more interesting. Wipo, blessed with a more splendid subject, harnessed the classical panegyric of a ruler to his purpose as a preacher. Conrad's reign lent itself to panegyric: he won battles against his enemies and he put down rebels. Wipo claimed that the glorious deeds of a Christian ruler were worth preaching as well as eulogizing. The deeds of pagan heroes and tyrants had been celebrated; so had those of the kings of Israel. What sinful sloth it was to neglect the stories of Christian kings and emperors! A ruler had charge of the public good; Conrad had fulfilled his function so well that his death evoked more public lament than had ever been heard at an emperor's death before. Wipo draws the conclusion that the biographer is also an evangelist:

Our Catholic kings, the defenders of the faith, rule without fear of error, since they keep Christ's law and the peace which he handed down to us in his Gospel. Surely, therefore, to publish their good deeds in writing is nothing less than to preach the Gospel of Christ?

He safeguarded himself by adding that the bad deeds of rulers were worth recording as a warning.

Like Helgald, Wipo had to edit his data to some extent. Conrad showed less favour to the Church than had the Saxon emperors, his predecessors. His biographer achieved a remarkable feat in raising his *Life* to so high a level. Wipo wrote seriously. He avoided details which struck him as frivolous; there is no gossip, though he tells some stories characteristic of Conrad's behaviour to point his moral. He proved that a royal biographer could add his quota to the expanding Bible of the saints.

Conrad's *Life* might have served as a model for Henry III's biographer, had he found one. It was useless to the biographer of Conrad's grandson, Henry IV. This Henry's reign contrasted with his father's and grandfather's in every way. His father died while he was still a child. A troubled minority was followed by personal tragedy and disaster to the empire. His sons turned against him. His victories proved brittle. The biographers of Louis the Pious could dwell on the fact that Louis, throughout his misfortunes, always remained a dutiful son of the Church. Henry IV, on the contrary, was excommunicated and deposed by Pope Gregory VII. Henry had himself crowned emperor by his antipope, after driving Gregory out of Rome. But it was a last resort; his antipope was just the ecclesiastical head of the imperialist party. The standard end to an emperor's reign was the glorious succession of his son and heir. Henry's heir was a rebel when the old emperor died, in the midst of such calamities that death came as a release.

It must have taken courage to write the *Life of Henry IV*. His biographer had no precedents. He could not present his subject either as a conqueror or as a holy or even a wise man, since his policies failed. No amount of editing would suffice to make his data fit the pattern. Nor would it have improved Henry's image to present him as the victim of a papal plot. That would have involved blackening Gregory VII. Gregory made many enemies; but Urban II was more politic, and opinion was veering back to the papal side when Henry died in 1106. A cautious approach to the Investiture Contest was called for.

An anonymous author undertook to apologize for the emperor. We know only that he moved in the imperial circle towards the end of Henry IV's reign and that he wrote soon after Henry's death. He had a good knowledge of the

Latin classics, of the Bible and of hagiography, so he was probably a clerk. His *Life* takes the form of a funeral lament. Henry's people mourn him; he had kept their sympathy through thick and thin. The writer calms his personal grief for his master by giving vent to his feelings. The imperial honour, exalted by Henry's forbears, had been trampled underfoot. That was cause for grief. Why did it happen? Not as a result of Henry's sins. He sowed his wild oats in his youth and afterwards lived virtuously. The Anonymous found the historical cause in the troubles of Henry's minority. Internal decay set in. Powerful men grew accustomed to snatch and grab. Peace never suited them for long, because it checked their ambitions. Hence revolt broke out as soon as the ruler had established law and order. A human cause accounted for the rebellions of Henry's sons. His enemies suborned them with promises and played off the natural resentment of youth against age.

The Anonymous went more deeply into the problem of causation than Thegan had done in his *Life of Louis the Pious*. Modern historians would like to go back further still and discover why German politics deteriorated during Henry's minority; but the work leaves them guessing. His biographer cheated a little by writing up Henry's few successes. His penitence at Canossa is represented as a diplomatic *coup*. He stole a march on his enemies by going to Gregory VII to receive absolution, exchanging a blessing for a curse, and returning to Germany to quell the rebels. It was certainly a clever move on Henry's part, though not quite as successful as the Anonymous makes out. It still remained to explain why Henry could never enjoy his victories. Defeat dogged his footsteps. The Anonymous plays down Henry's antipapal policies and does not criticize Gregory VII openly. The notion of Fortune's Wheel answered his problem. Fortune turned Henry's defeats into victories and then swiftly cast him down. German scholars put forward diverse opinions on Fortune's role in the *Life of Henry IV*. Her role can be interpreted as introducing a global view of history. Boethius' picture of the fickle goddess combined with a nordic concept of Fortune as inherent in the tribal chief, whose defeat meant loss of good luck for the whole people. Henry's troubles become all the more dreadful on this view. Another, less extreme, opinion is that the Anonymous appealed to Fortune as a subsidiary cause. He does not tell us that he means to write his book on the theme. The *Life* does not serve to illustrate Fortune's role. On the contrary, she is used simply to give pathos and drama to what might otherwise have looked like a history of petty quarrels and inconclusive fighting. She heightens our sense of tragedy. I prefer the second opinion; but in any case the Anonymous was an artist, who composed a touching tribute to Henry. Although he did not plan to write history in the strict sense of the word, he pondered the problems of causation.

Queens had their biographies, too. The most colourful is the *Encomium of Queen Emma. Encomium* is a modern title, but it expresses the writer's intention to praise her. Queen Emma, widow of the English King Aethelred and wife of the Danish King Cnut, commissioned a book in praise of herself and her family from a writer who was either a canon of St Omer or a monk of the neighbouring abbey of St Bertin, then in Flanders, now in the Pas-de-Calais. Emma's father was a duke of Normandy, and she spent three years of her life in Flanders. She knew that St Omer had a literary tradition: a canon or monk from there would make a good propagandist. Her career bristled with difficulties for a eulogist, especially as he was writing in her life-time, between 1040 and 1042. A queen ought to have the womanly virtues of being a loving wife and mother. Emma married twice – the second time to her first husband's deadliest enemy. She agreed as part of the bargain that her sons by Aethelred should forgo their claim to the English crown in favour of the sons she would bear to Cnut. It looked as though she was doing well for herself by neglecting her elder children. In fact they had slender chances of succeeding anyway.

The Anonymous suppressed all mention of Emma's first marriage. He gives us to understand that she was not a widow when Cnut sought her as a bride, and that her sons by Aethelred were the younger sons of her second marriage. That was why they had no claim against Cnut's offspring. Many readers might be expected to know the truth, so the Anonymous chose his wording carefully; no one could catch him out in a downright lie. The same technique was applied in other parts of his book where he had an interest in distorting the facts. He trots out the cliché in his preface that the historian must tell the truth, and then interprets it skilfully to mean 'nothing but the truth', though not 'the whole truth'. When he had no reason to mislead, he gave as correct and impartial a picture of the English scene as a foreigner, relying on hearsay, could do.

43 The Anonymous of St Omer presents his *Encomium* to Queen Emma. Her two sons Hardacnut and Edward stand beside her. From a manuscript of the mid-eleventh century which belonged to the abbey of St Augustine, Canterbury. *London, British Museum, MS Add. 33241, f.1v*

Emma herself disappears behind a cloud of rhetorical borrowings; but her eulogist could write vividly of what he had seen in person, as when he describes Cnut's generosity and devotion on his visit to St Omer. His famous pictures of naval scenes derive both from his reading of Virgil and from his powers of imaginative reconstruction. He had probably heard a description of a Viking fleet, though he may not have seen one. It caught his fancy, and there were classical precedents for describing ships. His two pictures of Viking fleets, dazzling the eye with their gilded prows and coloured boards, shine out from his pages. The centaurs and dolphins carved on the prows have slipped in from his reading; the dragons and bulls seem authentic enough, and so does the magic raven banner of the Danish fleet.

Drama, romance and brilliant writing are all absent from the *Life of Louis the Fat* by Abbot Suger of St Denis (d. 1151). We come down to humdrum life, centred on the small stage of the Île-de-France. Louis VI (1108–37) had more to his credit than Robert the Pious; he was a 'safe second-class' king. His main work for the French monarchy lay in subjecting the rebel barons of the royal domain. His forward policies in Normandy and Flanders misfired. Suger, however, was a propagandist of genius. He waved his wand over small beer and it turned into sparkling champagne. The magic came from St Denis, patron of Suger's abbey and of the French royal family. Suger was a great administrator of his abbey lands, a great church-builder and decorator and the king's right-hand man. He stressed Louis' role as lay patron and standard-bearer of St Denis. The king showed his devotion to St Denis from his boyhood onwards; he wished to be buried in the abbey church, unlike his father Philip I, who felt himself unworthy of such an honour. Suger found him a place. The *Life* ends with his burial there.

Suger gets his effect by statement rather than hyperbole. Why botch up a picture of Louis as a saint? It sufficed that he fought for St Denis, displaying the kingly virtue of 'strenuousness' in protecting his people against their enemies. The abbot exaggerates when he claims that Louis never overreached himself, but he does let him say at the end of his reign that he could have achieved more than he had. The supreme test came in 1124, when the German emperor, Henry V, threatened to invade France. Louis summoned his vassals to follow him in defence of the kingdom. Surprisingly, given the slightness of his hold, most of them either

44 Opposite: Christian rulers. The gilded copper cover of the *Golden Book* of the abbey of Prüm shows Christ in majesty worshipped by the Carolingian dynasty: Pippin and Charlemagne (above) and their descendants, Louis the Pious, Lothair, Louis the German and Charles the Bald. The rulers offer a church, a book; and charters recording donations to churches. The book is a cartulary, which includes genealogical tables of the Carolingian, Saxon and Salian kings, made about 1100. *Trier, Stadtbibliothek, Cod. 1709*

answered the summons or at least sent excuses. The emperor turned back with his tail between his legs. It appears from the German sources that he planned to make a punitive raid, not a large-scale invasion, and that he retreated partly because of a revolt in his rear. But Suger presents it as a splendid victory for the French against the Germans. St Denis had triumphed in the person of King Louis. Suger shared in his glory as abbot of St Denis and as the counsellor and biographer of his royal master.

We can see continuity and development in this sequence of royal biographers. In the first place, none of them undertakes to give us many facts and dates: these are 'not on the menu'. The practical Suger is the most generous. The classical eulogy and the Christian tradition of saints' *Lives* combined to reduce the amount of factual information required in biography. The Suetonian model permitted more precision, but it proved to be too bare for medieval taste. The rhetorical tradition defeated it. We cannot expect to find objectivity either; biographers wanted to praise or excuse. Their saving grace is that they remember the traditional advice to the historian to tell the truth and to report events as an eye-witness whenever possible. They generally keep the truth in sight, preferring to sin by omission and selection rather than by outright lying. Sudden flashes of realism light up their most conventional stories. If we judge them as propagandists, we have to admire their ingenuity. All do their best for rulers who fell short of what was expected of a Christian hero.

The development is clear and meaningful. The Church takes over biography. Einhard's Charlemagne stands alone. The ruler comes to be judged and presented to us in accordance with the standards approved by churchmen. We admire a devout emperor in Louis the Pious, a Christian king in Alfred, a saint in Robert the Pious, an evangelist in Conrad, generous donors to churches in Emma and Cnut, and the standard-bearer of St Denis in Louis VI. The unlucky Henry IV is neither anti-clerical nor anti-papal.

We see the same development when we turn from biography to less specialized kinds of historiography. The writers are churchmen, who see history through clerical glasses, but the general historian did not work to the same stereotype as the biographer. We shall find more diversity of interest and many more ways of treating the matter of history. There are surprises in store for us.

6

History, chronicle and historical scholarship
c. 950–c. 1150

Historiography, apart from annals, stopped on the Continent between the late ninth and early tenth centuries. The wars which resulted from the break-up of the Carolingian empire and raids by Vikings, Hungarians and Saracens made literary composition difficult. Then suddenly a first-class scholar appeared in Flodoard, canon of Rheims (d. 966). Flodoard was an industrious annalist; but he also wrote a *History of the Church of Rheims* and a poem on the triumphs of Christ and his saints. Like Bede, he was a scholar-historian. Both aimed to be more enterprising than mere compilers when they studied the history of the remote past; both wrote in clear Church Latin in order to reach as wide a public as possible. Flodoard collected evidence for the early history of Rheims, drawing on oral reports, classical Latin writers and saints' *Lives*. More, he looked at archaeological remains and he copied inscriptions. The dossier which he made in preparation for writing has been discovered recently. It shows how far afield he went in his search for evidence: he procured a copy of an inscription on an altar in a church in the Vosges, because a former archbishop of Rheims had dedicated the church. A visit to Rome enabled him to transcribe epitaphs on papal tombs for his poem. On the later history of Rheims Flodoard gave a careful account of what he knew from experience.

The next surprise is what I can only call '*salon* history', incongruous as it sounds. Liudprand, Widukind and Richer were all three classicists, entertainers and partisans. They wrote in classicizing Latin. Liudprand sprinkled his Latin with Greek words and phrases. His modern English translator had the happy idea of translating them into French, which gives an effect of politeness. Widukind and Richer both prefer classical 'temples' to 'churches' and call contemporary armies 'legions'. They refrain from quoting Scripture as a rule; Liudprand uses biblical phrases only when he has to describe an ecclesiastical occasion, just as he would wear vestments in church. They seem to have no 'sense of crisis', although they

45 The emperor Otto I presents a model of the cathedral church of Magdeburg to Christ in majesty. Otto founded and endowed the archbishopric of Magdeburg to forward mission work and conquest on his eastern border. He obtained a papal bull of foundation after his imperial coronation at Rome in 962. Detail of an ivory relief from Milan or Reichenau, about 970. *New York, The Metropolitan Museum of Art, Gift of George Blumenthal, 1941*

all lived through grim events, not as onlookers, but as men committed to a point of view in politics. The fact that they recount legends does not make them naïve, any more than Livy is naïve when he tells tales of early Rome. Liudprand's dirty stories recall Voltaire.

Liudprand (d. 972) began his career as a page at the court of King Hugh of Italy, and later passed into the service of Otto I, to whom he owed his bishopric of Cremona. He called his first book *Tit for Tat*, since he wrote it partly to avenge himself on his enemies. It is dedicated to a Spanish bishop. They had met at the court of Otto in Germany, and the bishop had suggested to Liudprand that he should write a history of his own times. He explains in his preface that he aims at amusing his readers. The study of philosophy calls for recreation in the form of comedy or of pleasing histories of heroic men. Students tired of the difficult perusal of Cicero will 'find refreshment in these outpourings of mine'. His spite against his opponents in Italian factions adds to our enjoyment of his *chronique scandaleuse*. So do his snide comments: 'The Italians like to have two masters, so that they can play off one against the other.' Liudprand, though a Lombard, wanted only one master, and that was Otto. His two shorter pieces are the *Deeds of Otto*, where he praises the emperor and blackens the anti-imperialist party, and *The Embassy to Constantinople*. This is a satirical memoir of his embassy to the Byzantine court; he disliked the Greeks and their food and manners and pretensions. His mud-slinging did lasting harm. It is only recently that historians have begun to question his shocking picture of the anti-imperialist factions at Rome. Popes and women are always news: the combination has proved irresistible.

Widukind preferred battles to court intrigue. He was a monk of the Saxon abbey of Corvey, a royal foundation, and was related to the German ruling family. He dedicated his *Deeds of the Saxons* to a nun-princess, Matilda, a daughter of Otto I. It is divided into three books, each having a preface more flattering than the last. Widukind proposes to entertain Princess Matilda and to increase her glory by glorifying her ancestors. He begins with the origins of the Saxons and goes down to Otto's death in 973. We do not know when Widukind died; the dates of the various recensions of his books are still controversial; but it seems that he began to write during Otto's lifetime. His picture of the Saxons represents a blend of German heroic tradition with the

Carolingian tradition handed down by Einhard. Widukind adds his personal version of the ancient Roman tradition. Henry the Fowler and Otto I are made to look like legendary heroes. They stand out larger than life as mighty warriors and hunters, generous as 'gift-givers' to their fighting men. Widukind's portrait of Otto owes something to Suetonius and Einhard. Otto, like Augustus Caesar, turned to the business of making 'divine and human laws' after defeating his domestic and foreign enemies.

The original feature of Widukind's *Deeds* was his revival of a post-Suetonian type of Caesar. He brought in the soldier-emperors of late antiquity, who owed their creation to the army. These were not civilians like the Caesars of the *Twelve Lives*. Widukind states that first Henry the Fowler and then Otto were acclaimed emperor on the battlefield, each after his greatest victory. Their historian gives each one the imperial title after his acclamation by the army. He ignores the facts, which must have been known to a man so close to the royal house, that Henry was not crowned as emperor and that he never used the title, while Otto waited until after his coronation at Rome in 962; he did not use the title regularly before then, even after his triumphant victory on the Lechfeld in 955. Widukind goes on to ignore Otto's imperial coronation by the pope in Rome. It was a wilful omission. He certainly knew that it had happened, and had no such scruple in recording Otto's victories over the rebellious Romans. The Princess Matilda would have known of it too. Widukind covers up his omission by warning her that he does not mean to tell her the full story of her father's deeds. It seems odd that he should have omitted the coronation at Rome and yet have described Otto's coronation by the archbishop of Mainz at Aachen, when he succeeded Henry the Fowler in 936. The reason must be that Widukind disliked the Roman connection. Perhaps Einhard encouraged his feeling that a heroic war-leader ought not to be crowned by a priest, even if that priest were the successor of St Peter. Otto had earned his title on the battlefield and did not need to have it conferred on him by a churchman. The royal coronation at Aachen fitted in better: it strengthened the link between Otto and Charlemagne.

The significance of Widukind's omission has been much discussed. His text lends itself to various interpretations, just as Einhard's secular bias can have more or less importance read into it. The real point is that Widukind explored a new area of ancient history, the period of soldier-emperors. He found a setting for the Saxons which would preserve their links with the Caesars without sacrificing their glory as war-leaders.

Richer (d. *c.* 998) was a monk of St Remigius of Rheims and had studied under Gerbert, later Pope Sylvester II; Gerbert was the best master of the Latin classics available in his day. Richer dedicated his *Histories* to Gerbert as his admiring pupil, and shows his sophistication by not apologizing or explaining his purpose, as was customary. Gerbert had asked for the book and thereby showed that he regarded historiography as a civilized pursuit. One did not need to apologize for imitating Julius Caesar. Richer followed Caesar in starting with a geographical account of Gaul; then he described the manners and customs of the inhabitants and sketched their early history. He treated the history of Gaul in detail after 888, the year of the final break-up of the Carolingian empire. Unfortunately for the repute of classicizing history, Richer's credibility is low. We can see him at work and watch his method. At first he relied on the scholarly Flodoard as his source, since Flodoard's writings were to hand at Rheims; Richer says so himself. He rewrote Flodoard so as to 'improve' the plain style, messing up the content as it pleased him. When his source gave out, he was able to write as a near contemporary and then as an eye-witness; but we distrust him already. He had a political bias. Friendship and interest led him to support Hugh Capet against the last French Carolingians. Worse still, his learning led him astray. He showed off his knowledge of medicine by inventing diseases for his characters to die of. At least, he has been accused of doing so; we cannot check him. His use of Sallust *can* be checked, and the result is discreditable. His fondness for the Roman historian induced him to change the season of a siege because he wanted to quote from the *Jugurthan War*. He makes Hugh Capet 'establish laws and make decrees' on his election as king in 987. The early Capetians were not legislators. All they did in that line was to authorize land transactions. But the Roman Caesars made laws, and so did the Ottos: Hugh Capet had to wear the toga to compete with them. Modern attacks on his *Histories* would have struck Richer as the crassest kind of pedantry. Like Liudprand and Widukind, he was a gifted story-teller, especially when he described his personal adventures; he is a good entertainer.

46 Opposite: the opening page of Richer's *History*, with his dedication to Gerbert, later Pope Sylvester II. This is one of the very few autograph copies of a medieval historical text to survive; the notes and corrections are in Richer's hand as well. *Bamberg, Staatsbibliothek, MS hist. 5, f.1r*

DOMINO AC BEATISSIMO PATRI GERBERTO REMORUM
ARCHIEPISCOPO. RICHERVS MONACHVS

Gallorum congressib; in uolumine regerendis imperii
pat scississime. G. auctoritas seminarium dedit. q
sum̃a utilitate affert. & rerum materia sese multiplici
probal. coanimi nisu complector. qua tuberis mira benig
nitate prebehor. Cui rei initium auicino sumens dece
res multo ante gestas. d. m. hincmari ante te forensi
remorum metropolitan. suis annalib. copiosissime an
nexui. Tantoq; supriora lector extinueniet. quanto
anteriori opusculi exordio perlegras̃set. Et hoc inqua ne
Karolorum aliorumq. frequens et unusq; opere reperitio
operis utrusq. ordine turbal. Vbi eni rerum ordo non
aduertitur. tanto nocentior error effunditur. quanto a serie ordinis
erratum seducitur. Vnde et hic aeq; illic sepe karoli. sepe
ludouici notis offerunt. preopere auctorum prudens lector
pregressaq; uoces pnotabit. Quorum reportib. bella a gallis
sepe numero patrata uariasq; eorum tumultus. ac diuer
sas negotiorum rationes. admemoria reducere scripto
specialiter propositum e. Siqua ut aliorum efferant pro
dentis rationes que ctam reportauerunt ad euo nisso
prouec. Inducendo queam presens effluere. plurima
sucenture credit. Re totius exordio narrationis
aggrediar. ut orbis terra orbis diuisione. galliaq;
in partes distributa. eoqd eius populorum moresac
actus describere proposui sit. EXPL PROLOG

Sedsi ignore antiquitatis. argumens ex quodam flodoardo presb
remensi libello. me alei̇de sumpsisse. non inepte dixero. Sed aliud
saltes altissimo opere iactionis umea. res ipsa euidentis
sime demonstrat. Sicq; lectori fieri arbitror me complacitur. ac
ad oma dixerim pollicetur RIN

To add to the *salon* illusion we have a woman historian, Hrotswitha, a nun of Gandersheim in Saxony. Students of medieval drama know her for her Christian adaptations of the comedies of Terence. She also wrote a historical poem on Otto I soon after his coronation at Rome in 962. Learned authors were rare at the time; an authoress was unique. Yet there she is in the masculine company of the *Patrologia Latina*, and a scent wafts up from the pages. Hrotswitha wrote in a light, tripping style. Her verses survive in fragments only; but enough remains to show that she felt a sentimental attachment to Christian Rome. What most attracted her to Otto was his love story: he rescued Queen Adelheid from her brutal oppressor, married her and reigned with her as his empress. Hrotswitha's poem is a 'real life romance'.

To taste a contrast with these literary historians we must turn to a monastic chronicle. Benedict, monk of St Andrew's by Monte Soracte (to the north-east of Rome), whose chronicle breaks off incomplete at 972, shows what passed for Latin in less learned circles. A scandalized German scholar has described his diction as 'the lowest to which the tongue of Cicero has ever sunk'. Old-fashioned country grammar – 'them's us's' – would sound just as odd if translated into Latin. Benedict had no use for rules, and he used dialect words. His copyist may have committed some of the gaffes, but the original cannot have been perfect. The very harshness of the style suits the story. We have seen Otto through the admiring eyes of Liudprand, Hrotswitha and Widukind. Benedict tells what it felt like to be conquered by the Saxon and plundered by his men of iron. His lament for 'the Leonine City', taken over by foreigners, has a suggestion of keening. It is more poignant than literature.

Historiography loses its rarity value during the eleventh century. More monks wrote chronicles; the papal biographers broadened out; their interests ceased to be local. All the genres handed down to the Middle Ages were cultivated, and hybrids were invented. We begin to see 'types', whereas the writers we have just met were 'originals'. Their successors do not show the same extremes of polish or roughness. They are not dull, however, since they react to the new movements of the period. The rise of the towns and the crusades must wait for later chapters. Here I shall choose a sample from the polemical histories of the Investiture Contest.

As we have seen, the Contest forced Henry IV's biographer to think about causes. Bruno wrote his book *On the Saxon War* as propaganda for the opposite side. Paradoxically, the most narrowly partisan of the polemical historiographers is the most thoughtful. Bruno belonged to the cathedral clergy of Magdeburg and knew the archbishop. On the latter's death he passed into the service of the bishop of Merseberg, to whom he dedicated his war history in 1082. 'Saxony for the Saxons' is Bruno's slogan. The Saxons rebelled against the Swabian Henry IV, who tried to 'enslave' them, as they saw it. They allied with Gregory VII for political reasons, not because they were reformers. Gregory's forgiveness of Henry at Canossa struck them as double-dealing. The pope had let them down. The Saxon rebels failed to win Gregory's full support for the antiking who had been elected to oppose Henry. Bruno came to dislike the pope and his legates almost as much as the Henricians. As freedom-fighters the Saxons ought to have won their wars. Their indifferent success made Bruno reflect on causes and collect evidence. First he had to justify their rebellion, a serious matter in the German Reich. Henry was a tyrant. Why? Like Henry's biographer, Bruno pointed to the minority as a cause, though he interpreted it differently. The young king was badly brought up by flatterers; he never mended his ways. Why did the Saxons suffer reverses? Perceptively Bruno blames them for breaking their promises to their Swabian allies by making a separate peace with Henry. This mistake on the Saxons' part split the common front for good and all. The blame after Canossa lay with Gregory VII, who encouraged the rebels, only to leave them in the lurch when it suited him. To substantiate his claim, Bruno assembled *pièces justificatives* in the form of the letters which passed between the pope and the Saxon princes and prelates. Gregory excused himself for absolving Henry; the Saxons bombarded him with reproaches and appeals for his moral backing: 'Come off the fence!' Bruno was well placed to get copies of the letters because of his connections with Magdeburg and Merseberg. There were precedents for inserting documents in ecclesiastical histories and chronicles, but *On the Saxon War* is a historical monograph on the model of *The Jugurthan War*: Bruno knew his Sallust. It was less usual to copy letters into literary history. His desperation led Bruno to mix his genres. His *Saxon War* was the better for it. Polemic stimulated heart-searching and novelty.

England had a national tradition of historical record. The *Anglo-Saxon Chronicle* is unique in the West as a sustained record of events written in the vernacular. It probably began to be compiled and to circulate soon after 899. Writers at various centres copied earlier versions and made additions. One version, the 'Peterborough Chronicle', was continued after the Norman Conquest down to 1155. Anglo-Norman men of letters put much of their creative energy into historiography. That is their distinctive contribution to the revival of learning in the twelfth century. My reason for treating them skimpily here is that the English-speaking student is well provided with good introductions and translations. I shall mention only the most famous names, Orderic Vitalis and William of Malmesbury.

These two men were contemporaries: both died in the early 1140s. Orderic had the longer life; he was born in 1075 and William some twenty years later. Both took monastic vows in their youth and remained monks of their abbeys, St Evroul in Normandy and Malmesbury respectively, throughout their careers. Both came of mixed parentage. William tells us that he came of an Anglo-Norman family; Orderic had a French or Norman father and an English mother. He was born near Shrewsbury, but his father brought him as a child oblate to St Evroul so that he might serve God undistracted by his kinsfolk (that is the reason Orderic gives for his removal to a foreign land). He revisited England to collect material for his *History*. We know that he stayed at Worcester and Crowland. Both Orderic and William were dedicated scholars and book-hunters, yet we have no evidence that they ever met or that they read each other's books. As historians they were as different as chalk from cheese. Orderic's *Ecclesiastical History* conjures up a picture of Clio, Muse of history, as a big fierce woman browbeating her votary. William understood how to keep his mistress under control.

Orderic presents himself to his readers as a simple monk. He did not hold office in his abbey and had few occasions to attend church councils or go to court. The *History* ends on a note of thanksgiving: the author rejoices that he has lived all his life in religion, spiritually, if not always physically, detached from the turmoil of the world. We get the impression of a modest man, who does not force himself on our notice except to authenticate his story as an eyewitness and to show us how his career fitted into his narrative. He mentions

> An. dccc li. Her forð ferde ælfheah bisc on pint on...
> An. dccc lii. Her norðhymbre fordrifan anlaf cyning. ⁊ under fengon ymb haroldes sunu.
> An. dccc liii.
> An. dccc liiii. Her norðhymbre fordrifon ymb. ⁊ eadred feng to norðhymbra rice.
> An. dccc lv. Her eadred cyning forðferde. ⁊ feng eadwig to rice eadmundes sunu. ⁊ aflæmde s dunstan ut of lande
> An. dccc lvi. Her forðferde wulfstan arceb.
> An. dccc lvii.
> An. dccc lviii.
> An. dccc lix. Her eadwig cyning forðferde on kl octobr. ⁊ feng eadgar his broðor to rice. On his dagum hit go dode georne. ⁊ god him geuðe þ he wunode on sibbe þa hwile þe he leofode. ⁊ he dyde swa him þearf wes ⁊ eaþmode

his ordination, his rare excursions outside his abbey, and his personal reactions to disasters: in the wreck of the White Ship (1120), when Prince William, son of Henry I, was drowned with all his company, none of Orderic's friends or relatives was involved; only common humanity makes him grieve for those who died. His asides echo the usual platitudes on the historian's task and the divine plan in history, though he can let shrewd comments fall from the lips of a seemingly gullible character. He blames robbers and spoilers of Church – especially monastic – property in the usual way. Hatred of cruelty in any form marks him out as being truly sensitive. His pity for victims and his condemnation of oppressors, even those whom he admired, are more than mere claptrap.

Ironically enough, Clio tricked him into recording the deeds of the Normans, the most violent and restless people of his time. He did not start with the intention to do so. His abbot asked him to write a history of St Evroul. He set out to give an account on traditional lines of the founders, bene-factors, privileges, growth, prosperity, misfortunes and losses of his abbey. But this took him further afield. Orderic felt obliged to include the history of Norman families whose members had contacts with the monastery. Then he realized that he had to write a history of the duchy, which he could not separate from the history of all the Normans. The

47 The Peterborough version of the *Anglo-Saxon Chronicle* with entries for the years 951–959. Additions have been made in blank spaces. *Oxford, Bodleian Library, MS Laud. misc. 636, f.36r*

Normans had conquered and settled in Neustria; Normans from the duchy conquered and founded states in southern Italy and Sicily; Duke William conquered the kingdom of England. Normans from the duchy and Italy played a leading part in the First Crusade. Bohemond of Sicily carved out a principality for himself at Antioch. Family and religious ties persisted wherever the Norman network spread. 'In for a penny, in for a pound': the *Ecclesiastical History* turned into a history of Christendom. The author worked on several parts of it concurrently, bringing it up to 1141, when he felt too tired at the age of sixty-seven to hold his pen any longer. At an earlier stage he had compiled a 'world history' from the Incarnation up to his own day to serve as a preface and make his work as comprehensive as possible.

Changes of plan as he went along necessitated digression and repetition. Orderic excuses himself when an extra long digression has led him right off the rails. The monastic mode of writing encouraged him to make a virtue of necessity. Monastic homilists proceeded by digression; it belonged to the technique of 'holy reading'. The idea that one should make a scheme before starting and keep to it when writing would have struck a monk as misguided. St Gregory says so in his *Morals on Job*, one of the most widely read books of the Middle Ages:

... if a river, as it flows along its channel, meets with open valleys on its side, into these it immediately turns the course of its current, and when they are copiously supplied, presently it pours itself back into its bed. Thus should it be with everyone who treats of the Divine Word.

The historian aimed at edification. It suited his purpose to turn aside in order to tell of a saint's life and miracles or to describe the conversion of a heathen people to Christianity.

Orderic had qualms nevertheless. He meant to write ecclesiastical history, but it encroached on secular. He tried to distinguish between the two genres and it worried him that he could not do full justice to the latter:

Skilful historians could write a memorable history of these great men and women. . . . We, however, who have no experience of the courts of the world, but spend our lives in the daily rounds of the cloisters where we live, will briefly note what is relevant to our purpose.

William the Conqueror's children 'left abundant material for eloquent and learned men to compose mighty tomes'. The

History offers us more than brief notes on Anglo-Norman political history, in spite of his disclaimer. But they did not satisfy him; he thought that the story needed telling afresh in its own right and not as a mere annex to church history. The historian had inexhaustible opportunities: Orderic could not pursue all of them.

The Normans should have thanked him for the space he gave them, limited though it was. They appeared in historiography as a Christian people for the first time. Orderic's Norman predecessors had dealt with isolated aspects of Norman history; Dudo of St Quentin, for example, told a partly legendary story of the conquest of Normandy. In general non-Norman historians continued to portray Normans as ninth- and tenth-century writers had done, as cruel barbarian invaders of Christian kingdoms. Orderic had no illusions as to their national traits. He makes the Conqueror describe the men of his duchy as 'a turbulent people, ever ready to cause disturbances'. They are 'ever restless and desirous of visiting foreign lands'. Victorious abroad, they fall to cutting one another's throats as soon as a strong ruler is removed. But they excel as fighters and church builders. Orderic's lifelong sense of being an Englishman abroad was compatible with a preference for the Normans against their neighbours, Angevins, Flemish and French in the north, Greeks and Italians in the south and east. He had a standard rule of conduct to apply to churchmen; in telling secular history his prejudices overcame him. His own experience made him aware of the differences between the men of Normandy and their enemies on the border. He wrote as a partisan of the Normans.

The result was a new 'barbarian history' set into the framework of his *Ecclesiastical History*. The pagan Norsemen perform heroic feats of arms; then their prowess as Christians is recorded, though Orderic does not suppress their evil deeds. The substance of his *History* has an original element; he broke new ground.

Otherwise Orderic is 'the modern researcher's historian'. His vast, untidy narrative supplies a wealth of information on all kinds of subjects. Many details are incorrect, since his sources misled him, although he made painstaking efforts to get at the facts by reading chronicles and charters and asking questions of persons likely to know what happened. On the other hand, his classical studies do not get in his way when he records contemporary behaviour. There were no recognized types on which to model French châtelains and Norman lords of middling wealth and moderate piety. Orderic presents them as real individuals, as he observed them. We have come a long way from '*salon* history'.

Apart from its interest for local history, the *Ecclesiastical History* mirrors the history of ideas. It reflects what a Black Monk thought of the new reformed orders. Orderic disliked 'Cistercian novelties', but he tried to be fair. He is also a source for the history of political theory. He shows us what a monk of a Norman monastery expected of rulers. Strong government was essential to quell in-fighting and invasions. Orderic assumed that rebels must always be in the wrong. They put their private interest before the public good. A ruler who burdens his subjects with taxes and who snaps his fingers at clerical privilege is a lesser evil; far worse is the ruler who absents himself and neglects to discipline his barons. Orderic states a common monastic view of government; but he puts it forcibly and backs it by examples. He had plenty to hand: rebellions broke out frequently in Normandy.

The *Ecclesiastical History* is a long haul, but it rewards persevering readers by showing them how the world looked as seen from the cloisters of St Evroul. William of Malmesbury, on the contrary, is 'a modern historian's historian'. We read him as a source of facts and ideas, as we read Orderic; but we study his method too. William resembles Flodoard. He followed Flodoard unconsciously and Bede quite consciously in holding the study of the past to be a discipline in its own right: it meant far more labour than the mechanical up-ending of earlier histories and chronicles. Intensive research into the records of past ages was called for. William started with the same advantage as Orderic: the abbey library at Malmesbury housed a good store of books, since a scholar-abbot from Jumièges in Normandy had refounded it. William held the office of librarian. His duties gave him the chance to browse there and to acquire new texts for the library. He supplemented the written sources available on the history of Britain by collecting oral information both locally and on journeys round the country. He interviewed men who had seen or who had had handed down to them 'things in danger of being forgotten'. He entered a *caveat* for data which he could not verify. He tried to distinguish between legend and history. Naturally he swallowed some fiction and fable as factual, but not everything that came his way. Tall stories concerning King Arthur of Britain were circulating while he wrote. They did not deceive him – partly, it is true, because twelfth-century Welshmen struck him as unlikely to have had such valiant ancestors as the Arthur stories supposed. William made a more self-conscious effort than Orderic to judge and criticize his material.

William is more analytical and more interested in motive as a historian. He enjoys comparing a person's avowed motives for acting as he did with his real ones. To deduce motives involves guessing. William guessed, as historians still do. He worked on the principle that men normally act from motives of self-interest. We should look at their interest and not believe their professions. Pope Urban II proclaimed the First Crusade at the Council of Clermont, in order to help the Christians in the East and to win salvation for men's souls. The pope's true motives, according to William, were 'less well-known'. Urban hoped that the general confusion resulting from the crusade would enable him to recover the papal lands in Italy, which had been lost to the imperialists in the Investiture Contest. William based his interpretation on gossip or on his own view of what was probable; the Council of Clermont took place when he was still a baby or not yet born. But the guess at Urban's motives shows how he looked for historical causes.

To act 'without self-interest' seemed to William rare and wonderful. He records disinterested loyalty as the exception. Earl Robert of Gloucester supported the Empress Matilda, his half-sister, against King Stephen in the civil wars consistently, unlike her many fair-weather friends. His motive was sheer loyalty to her. Crediting readers with his own scepticism, William doubts whether they will believe his statement that the earl acted unselfishly. He doubts it all the more because they will know that the earl was his patron. He defends himself against the charge of flattery in order to prove that his statement is true. *Cui bono?*, 'to whose benefit?', remains a favourite question asked by historians when they discuss why men behaved in a certain way. William asked it and supplied the answers as a student of human nature, who looked at the seamy side first.

His sense of form was surer than Orderic's. William made a better show of separating sacred from secular history. His *Deeds of the Bishops* represents an ecclesiastical history of England, his *Deeds of the Kings* the equivalent in secular history. On reaching his own time he ran the usual risk of offending persons who were still alive if he told the truth.

Orderic, sheltered in his cloister, had less reason to fear that great men would notice what he wrote of their behaviour. William had more contact with princes. He solved his problem by writing royal biographies of the Suetonian type, which enabled him to give a detached, schematic account of rulers without judging them. He handled his model skilfully, and living individuals do come through. Some guessing was in order. We cannot test William's statement that Henry I begot large numbers of bastards to serve as a prop to his throne rather than for pleasure; but it adds a nice touch to the portrait of a cold, calculating and clever king. William painted it with loving care. His last work was a historical monograph, the *New History*. It begins with an account of Henry I's last years, leading up to the civil wars of Stephen's reign. William left it unfinished at his death in 1143. It is his best piece. Here he could exploit his knowledge as an eyewitness of events in south-west England and draw on contemporary evidence. He is careful to tell us when he was present on the occasions which he describes and when he relies on hearsay. Robert of Gloucester, Stephen's leading opponent, was the hero and recipient of the book; we are in the thick of politics.

William took seriously the precept that the historian should be impartial. He writes proudly that on account of his mixed parentage he can take an impartial view of the Norman conquest of England. Unfortunately he goes on to give the official Norman version with its bias against Harold and its blackening of the English Church. The same goes for Orderic, in spite of his awareness of being English. It was the only version to hand. William's boast witnesses to his ideal of impartiality. It was unattainable. His sources took sides, and he followed. The *New History* put his theories to the test. He invented his own version of the civil wars as he went along, having no source to guide him. He survives the test very well. The *New History* gives as fair a picture of the characters involved and the causes of the wars as could be expected from a declared partisan of Gloucester. It is a mark of his skill in the historian's craft that William puts his cards on the table. He credited students of history with the desire to read an impartial account and he tried to satisfy them by explaining where he stood, so that they could make allowances.

His gifts as a scholar justify William's popularity with modern historians: he strikes them as 'a chap like us' or 'almost a colleague'. The joy of shaking hands across the centuries may have led to some exaggeration of his modernity as an investigator of the remote past and as an interpreter of the present; but our feeling of kinship with the Malmesbury historian is real. That he possessed the crowning talent of readability adds to his appeal. So did other Anglo-Norman historians; it was a characteristic trait; even Orderic is readable in moderate doses. The difference is that William provides more scholarship as well as more entertainment.

None of the writers reviewed in this chapter bothered his head about problems of periodization. An occasional reference to the current decline in morals and the approaching end shows us that an author accepted the tradition that he was living in the sixth age of the world. Historiographers settled down to foreseeing a future of indefinite length in this last age. Both Orderic Vitalis and Henry of Huntingdon (d. c. 1155), in his *History of the English*, claim that the study of history helps to predict the future and to understand new happenings as they occur. Orderic puts it explicitly:

It sometimes happens that many events present themselves to the ignorant as unheard-of things, and new circumstances are frequently occurring in modern times on which no light can be thrown to inexperienced minds except by reference to former transactions.

The monk of St Evroul and the archdeacon of Huntingdon both assume that the historian's foresight will range over home ground. The new occurrences are not imagined as apocalyptic. Both took an interest in the prophecies ascribed to the Welsh wizard Merlin, which were circulating when they wrote. Some had already come to pass; they belonged to the genre of 'prophecy after the event', though this was not realized; others might be fulfilled in the future. But Merlin's prophecies were political, treating of human battles and conquests. The excitement which they aroused suggests lack of interest in the coming of Antichrist. Curiosity centred on battles between the English kings and their neighbours, not on the approach of Doomsday.

But Orosius had not slipped quite out of mind. His panoramic view of history was still challenging. Historiographers read the *History Against the Pagans* as an authentic source for early history, to be copied as a prelude to their account of more recent events. But a thoughtful reader would find more in it. Orosius dared him to write a new universal history, lifting his eyes to far horizons. Could one bring Orosian periodization up to date? It was time to try.

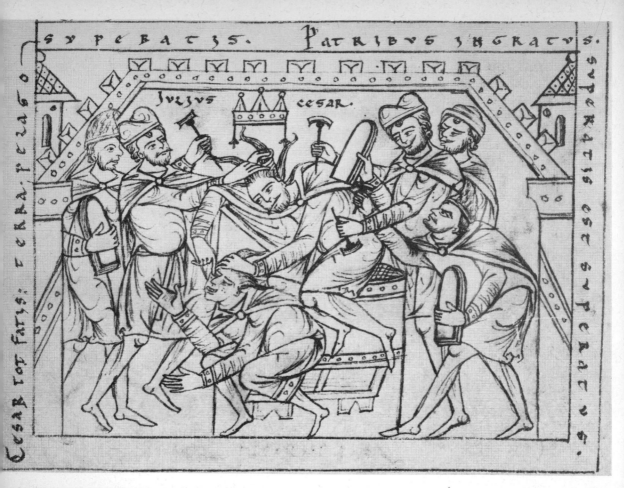

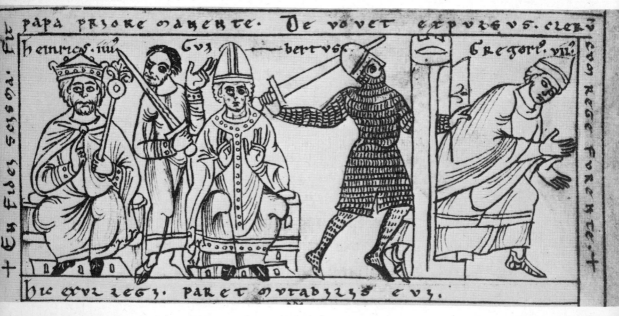

Universal history

Benedetto Croce rated 'reflective history' as the highest type of historiography. 'There are no periods in history, only problems.' The reflective historian examines problems. Universal history does not exist for any historian worthy of the name, because he cannot turn his mind to all aspects of history at once. Only a hack will write history at second or third hand, as one must if one tries to write universal history. While Croce's statements may be valid for modern historiography, they do not apply to that of the twelfth century. Granted that reflective history is the highest type, and that the true historian concerns himself with problems, he still cannot get away from periods. To write reflective history in the twelfth century meant reflecting on the periodization handed down by Orosius. That posed the problems. What was history if not universal? To deny its universality would have amounted to denying the truth of Christianity. But did the early time schemes of the six ages and the four monarchies provide the right framework for writing the history of the centuries between the fifth and the twelfth? Historians, chroniclers and biographers abounded; but no one had volunteered to be a new Orosius. The task bristled with difficulties.

The chief problem had its roots in the fact of change. There were philosophical reasons why 'change' meant decay. Change and decay afflict us from the moment of our conception in the womb. That belief belonged to St Augustine's philosophy of life. The parallel between the ages of the world and the life of man, with its rider that the world had reached the evening of the sixth age, made it natural to suppose that historical changes would normally be for the worse. It was easy to tell the tale of decline, easy and quite enjoyable; historiographers revelled in doling out blame. Changes for the better, on the contrary, called for explanation: how could they happen in a period of decline? Yet novelties sprang up on all sides. Some could be classified as 'bad', but not all; some were indisputably 'good', and therefore puzzling.

48, 49 Opposite: illustrations to the *History of the Two Cities* by Otto of Freising (see pp. 100–103), from a German manuscript of about 1170. The upper picture shows the murder of Julius Caesar. Roman senators, angry at his assumption of power, encourage his murderers to stab him. Caesar's death at the moment of triumph exemplifies the instability of worldly affairs. The lower picture shows recent history. Henry IV, a royal counsellor and the antipope Guibert (see p. 73) connive at the attempted murder of Pope Gregory VII, who is seen escaping from Rome. *Jena, Universitätsbibliothek, MS Bos.9.6., f.20v and 79r*

It is clear for all to see how many things, and things of great importance which are needed for this life, which are of use both to the good and to the bad, which are very beautiful in their own order, have been made and are being made both by good men and by wicked men. . . .

Hence derive in the realms of literature, art and architecture, through the countless discoveries of all sorts which men have made, so many branches of learning, so many kinds of professions, precisions in scientific research, arts of eloquence, varieties of positions and posts and innumerable investigations into the nature of this world.

What prospects these lines evoke! They were written by a Cistercian abbot called William of St Thierry, a devoted admirer of St Bernard, in his *Golden Epistle* to the Carthusian monks of Mont Dieu (1144–8). William and his friends had renounced the world; but he realized how stimulating it was to live in the world at such a time. No scholar of the early twelfth century could shut his eyes to the social, economic and intellectual changes taking place around him.

Economic developments of course led to abuses by wicked men. A churchman would disapprove of the rise of the towns and the townsmen's demand for privileges, which upset the God-given social order. Increasing wealth bred luxury and vicious fashions in clothes and hair-styles. Usury flourished. The 'varieties of positions and posts' mentioned by William of St Thierry evidently referred to the expansion of government, both ecclesiastical and secular. More sophisticated methods of extracting money from subjects led to more graft and oppression, as the officials enriched themselves. Lawyers and bureaucrats presented a new target for moralists. But who could deny that some of the new movements were 'good'? Churchmen rejoiced at the success of the First Crusade. The new religious orders, the Canons Regular of St Victor, the Cistercians or White Monks, Premonstratensians or White Canons, and communities of hermits, presented the seeker after perfection with a bewildering choice of ways to his goal. Religious reform in the early Middle Ages had been limited in scope to monks and hermits. Now the Black Monks had rivals. Members of each order claimed that its customs and ideals derived from the New Testament. More challenging still, student numbers had multiplied. There were more and better schools to provide education for a larger élite. Again, bad men abused their opportunities. Students were undisciplined; masters and students alike wasted their time on 'frivolous questions'. But study could serve the Church if it were rightly used. The schools equipped clerks to undertake pastoral care as well as deepening their understanding of Catholic doctrine.

Some scholars reflected on the fact of change, found it 'good', and gave improvement a place in their outlook on history. Hugh of St Victor (d. 1141), a Canon Regular who taught at the abbey of St Victor at Paris, had a unique and personal sense of historical development. He started from the traditional view of history as the history of salvation and drew the conclusion: the Church must encourage the growth of new institutions to meet new needs; how otherwise could she fulfil her mission on earth? 'Novelties', therefore, belonged to the divine plan. Godfrey of St Victor, one of Hugh's pupils, shared his master's optimism. His *Microcosmos*, a long theological treatise, shows how man, even fallen man, has been endowed with marvellous natural capacities to invent what he needs to live a full and civilized life on earth. Godfrey waxes as lyrical as William of St Thierry on the increased output of books on all kinds of topics.

50 Godfrey of St Victor, a pupil of Hugh, teaches at the abbey of St Victor at Paris. He holds his *Microcosmos*, which he composed about 1185. From a thirteenth-century French copy of the *Microcosmos. Paris, Bibliothèque Mazarine, MS 102, f.144r*

Anselm of Havelberg, a member of the new order of White Canons, defended the Canons against accusations of innovation. He did so on historical grounds. It was not enough to argue that the way of life he had chosen derived from the Gospel; he realized that to reform means to innovate; one cannot return to the values of the past at the present time without some kind of adaptation. Therefore, Anselm argued, the Holy Spirit continues to inspire new forms of religious life, even in the last age of the world. He grasped the nettle; changes for the better can happen even in the last age.

Novelties forced themselves on the notice of another group of scholars, the canon lawyers. This was a professional matter, which intruded into their teaching and practice. Canon law was developing as fast as theology. The rules governing cases judged in the Church courts and in the papal Curia increased in number and complexity. The substratum of canon law went back to the Bible, Church councils and papal decretals (with forgeries among them); but interpretations and new rulings to meet new problems were constantly added to the original basis. Canon lawyers worked *ex officio* on the corpus of canon law, old and new. They could not overlook the differences between the law they handled and the practices of the early Church. The rules on clerical celibacy and property-holding, for example, had no parallels in the New Testament. But they were necessary to cope with present-day society. A canonist would approve of the fact that Christian life was increasingly regulated by the Church and increasingly tied to the papacy. Professionals take pride in their work, especially when it makes them important. The canon lawyers believed strongly in their calling. It involved making and applying changes in the courts. They were not backward-looking or nostalgic for the past. Legal developments benefited the Church, or so they assumed in their teaching of canon-law books.

The scholars I have mentioned were theologians or canonists, not historians. Hugh of St Victor was the only one who wrote a history book. His book was a manual for the use of students of Arts and theology in the form of a universal chronicle. Hugh compiled it as a book for use in teaching; he did not treat it as a means to express his views on historical development. Historiographers were more conservative and more allergic to ideas than theologians or canonists. They recorded changes and novelties, with praise or blame as the case might be. Already the Burgundian historian Ralph Glaber (d. soon after 1049) had noted the current enthusiasm for church-building: the earth seemed to be putting on white garments. But he did not discuss the relevance of this change to the old age of the world.

The six ages were taken for granted. The time scheme of the four monarchies ought to have stimulated historiographers to think and criticize. This theory could be measured against actual fact. Periods exist in the mind, whereas a monarchy is concrete. Did the fourth world monarchy, the Roman, still exist? We left it in the seventh century, prolonging its life through Byzantine rule. Some historians held that it had already been divided up among lesser kings; others ignored it. Then Charlemagne's coronation gave the Roman empire a new lease of life. It marked a shift of power. Byzantine hold on Italy weakened. As Byzantine prestige declined, the popes turned to the Franks to protect them from both the Greeks and the Lombards.

A new theory was invented in Frankish court circles to justify the revival of empire in the West. The empire had been 'transferred to the Franks from the Greeks', without ceasing to be Roman. Hence the fourth monarchy lived on. The theory of 'transfer' had internal contradictions: the

Byzantine empire survived, and indeed was acknowledged by Charlemagne; the Carolingian empire had quite different boundaries from the Roman. The Roman empire centred on the Mediterranean, the Carolingian on the Rhineland. Such petty details weighed light in the scale. The concept of empire and the imperial title outlasted the break-up of the Carolingian empire. Otto I's coronation at Rome marked a further stage in the transfer theory. The Roman empire had been 'transferred to the Germans from the Franks'. After all, this was less surprising than transfer to the Franks from the Greeks; both Franks and Germans had barbarian origins.

The Saxon and later Salian empire looked less Roman than Charlemagne's. Its boundaries stopped short to the west of Flanders and Lorraine. France, Britain, the Spanish peninsula and southern Italy lay outside it. The Saxon and Salian emperors refrained from pressing their claims as emperors over their fellow-rulers. Hence the question of status hardly arose in practice. Rulers outside the effective bounds of the empire did not regard themselves as mere kinglets, in theory subjects of the empire. What did historians make of the situation? There was a conspiracy of silence. To take an example from England: Henry of Huntingdon in his *History of the English* (written about 1145) mentions the coronation of Charlemagne as emperor, but not Otto's. He and many others dealt with the fourth monarchy by omission. Nor did they ask whether it had been divided among ten kings, as foretold in Daniel's vision, and, if so, whether this heralded the coming of Antichrist.

One historian made a timid adjustment instead of merely ignoring the transfer theory. Hugh, a monk of Fleury, who died soon after 1117, began by writing an *Ecclesiastical History* on traditional lines. The transfer of empire to Charlemagne presented no difficulty to Hugh: he counted Charlemagne and the Franks as French. He finished his *History* at the division of the Carolingian empire among the sons of Louis the Pious. Next he wrote a history of the 'modern' kings of France from the death of Charlemagne to 1108. His plan faced him with the problem of the relations between the kings of France and the German emperors. Hugh claims that the French separated themselves from the Germans after the battle of Fontenoy, won by the French king Charles the Bald in 841: 'The kingdom of the Franks has remained separate and divided from the Roman empire from that day to this.' Hugh does not deny the continued existence of the Roman empire, now ruled by Germans; he simply registers the fact that the French kingdom does not belong to it. He seems to be meeting the challenge; then he stops half-way. It was inconsistent to accept the identification of the present-day empire with the fourth monarchy: the empire had ceased to be universal on his own showing.

It fell to a German to think out the problem. Otto of Freising stands alone in his glory as a reflective historian. Exceptional qualifications and experience fitted him for the task. Otto was born about 1115. He belonged to the German nobility, Babenberg on his father's side and Staufer on his mother's. The two families feuded, in spite of the marriage alliance between Otto's parents. The disorders in his country made a deep impression on him. The young nobleman went to study in Paris, where he read Arts and theology. Here he could watch academic feuds, and here too his loyalties were divided: he admired St Bernard and yet was friendly with Bernard's opponent, Gilbert of la Porrée. Then Otto joined the Cistercian order, St Bernard's. He became abbot of Morimond and then, at little more than twenty, bishop of Freising. He owed his quick promotion to his kinsmen, but he was learned and able. As a German aristocrat, a Paris scholar, a Cistercian monk and a bishop of the Reich, Otto had an individual outlook and a probing mind. His *History of the Two Cities*, written between about 1143 and 1145, brought Orosius up to date.

The title echoes St Augustine; Otto set out to write a history of the two cities, the heavenly and the earthly, described in the *City of God*. But St Augustine was an early casualty: Otto found that he had to identify the city of God with the Church. He saw Augustine's point that good and bad Christians mingled in the Church on earth; but a historian had to treat the Church as an institution after her recognition by Constantine; he had no choice. That left him with Orosius as his model for universal history. His *Two Cities* is a history of the Church and her enemies set into the time schemes of the six ages and the four monarchies. He dealt with the history of the Church as an institution by explaining that her state was 'happier' after gaining power and wealth than it had been during the persecutions in the early days, but not morally better. He enlarged the Orosian picture by adding the history of two other institutions, study and religion (by which he meant the religious orders). These counted as part of the history of the Church.

Looking for a key to the changes that had taken place since the time of Orosius, which would enable him to plot out the whole sweep of history, Otto pointed to movement from East to West. The centres of world power, political, intellectual and religious, arose in the East and moved westward. Their history fitted into the six ages: monarchy or empire, the Church, study and religion, each had its period of rise, apogee and decline within the span of each age in turn. In Otto's eyes, monarchy or empire was not the enemy of the Church. He took over from Orosius the belief in the Roman empire's positive role; it protected the Church. Her enemies were heretics, pagans and bad Christians, whether clerics or laymen. They attacked her in all ages.

To begin with world monarchy: Otto tidied up the Orosian picture by making parallels. The dual empire of the Medes and Persians corresponded to that of the Greeks and Franks. Empire was transferred to the Franks when first Charlemagne and then Otto I revived the Roman empire. Otto of Freising regarded the Franks and the Germans as one Teutonic people. Hence the transfer from one to the other was a domestic affair. He tried to find out which people held the empire in the dark days between the break-up of Charlemagne's empire and the coronation of Otto I. Perhaps it belonged briefly to the Lombards, another Teutonic people. Clearly, however, world monarchy had moved from the Oriental dynasties to the Greeks and the Romans and thence to the Germans, who had received the empire by transfer. It was still Roman. Clearly, too, a transfer was always followed by rise, peak and decline. The fate of Charlemagne's empire resembled that of the Orientals, and that of the Greeks and the Romans; so did that of the German empire. First, in each case, came rise by conquest, then a time of prosperity, and then defeat by enemies at home and abroad. The German empire rose by conquest; it reached its peak under Henry III; it declined under Henry IV. There was no recovery this time. Henry IV's defeat represented a victory for the Church. Otto quoted a prophecy from the statue dream in Daniel (2: 33–4) forecasting the unprecedented excommunication and deposition of an emperor by a pope. But the Church's victory did not compensate for the collapse of the secular power. Disorder reigned both in the empire and in 'other kingdoms'; he instanced the civil wars between Stephen and Matilda in England to prove that 'other kingdoms' had their troubles as well as the empire. What remained but to await the coming of Antichrist? Otto did not admit that the empire had been divided among the ten kings of Daniel's vision; but he thought it was doomed to disappear. He was not quite consistent in his treatment of the Western empire as a world monarchy; he gave the Byzantine ruler the title of emperor, and he referred to 'other kingdoms' without stating that their rulers belonged to the empire of the West. Otherwise his Orosian pattern made sense in political history. The Roman empire had indeed declined; the emperors could not even keep order within their boundaries.

'Study' proved less amenable to the pattern of rise and fall. Certainly it had been transferred from the East to the West. The idea went back to Alcuin, who told Charlemagne that he must found a 'new Athens' at his capital city of Aachen. As a matter of ancient history it was clear that the Greeks had inherited the wisdom of the East and transmitted it to the Romans. Now study flourished in France and learning tended to be concentrated in the schools of Paris. It seems likely that scholars at Paris were appropriating the theory of transfer of study. It corresponded to reality, since the cathedral schools of Germany and the Rhinelands had lost their attraction; scholars made straight for Paris if they wanted to study north of the Alps. Otto of Freising probably picked up the notion while studying at Paris. Hugh of St Victor may have influenced him.

The difficulty was that if the history of study followed the pattern of political history, then study must have fallen into decline. Rise, apogee and fall followed upon transfer. Otto may have judged that the heyday of the Paris schools had passed. What he says of contemporary studies is so ambiguous that it can be interpreted either way. He does not define his view precisely, as he does when writing of empire. In any case, study had moved closer to the Atlantic seaboard, which marked the end of the known world. Geographically, the schools could expand no further, however long the process of decline might be. A fourteenth-century Oxford poet predicted that study's next move would be to 'outside peoples, far to the West': he was probably joking.

'Religion' was more troublesome still. Otto despaired of the empire. He may have disapproved of Paris doctrines and teaching methods; perhaps that explains why he became a Cistercian. He had nothing but admiration for the new ascetic movements and their saints. He tried to apply his pattern to religion. It fitted into the beginning well enough.

Religion rose in the East; the Old Testament told of holy hermits. Christian monasticism originated with the Desert Fathers. Now it had moved westward. But far from declining, it throve anew. Light shone in the darkness. The *History of the Two Cities* dwells on the mutability of human affairs as manifested in earthly institutions. Religion differed from empire and study; the saints put themselves above mutability. Their merits upheld the tottering world: 'We should expect the world to end soon, were it not supported by the prayers and good works of holy men.' Otto may have had St Bernard in mind. He had joined St Bernard's order and he wrote before the abbot of Clairvaux had dimmed his reputation as a saint and wonder-worker by preaching the Second Crusade, which came to grief.

Religion flourished as it had no business to do. It overlapped untidily with Otto's time schemes. He yielded to the evidence, a merit rare in a historian so committed to a theory. He did not force the facts to lie down on his Procrustean bed. Religion might decline in the future; it showed a strange resilience in surviving its transfer to the West. It lagged behind the pattern of rise, apogee and fall. Otto had the honesty to acknowledge his difficulty. Honesty is what a reader of his *History* has come to expect. Otto had a strong critical sense and applied it to hallowed legends; he always wanted to pay due regard to the facts which he knew. This caution appears even in his last book, which is not history but 'meta-history'. It deals exclusively with the supernatural. Otto outlines the Last Things; mutability gives way to eternity. But even here he draws his data from the Bible and the Fathers without obtruding his speculations.

Otto was an untypical historian. The *History of the Two Cities* hardly circulated outside Germany. Historiographers did not imitate his 'reflective' history. Theologians, lawyers and publicists continued to discuss the relations between the empire and papacy and between the empire and other kingdoms. The theme of the transfer of study from East to West had a long life. But no historian after Otto tried to knit the transfer theory into the pattern of universal history. None of them tackled the problem of changes for good in the old age of the world. Was it due to laziness, myopia or conservatism? It is impossible to say.

Otto himself may have scrapped his theory of universal history in later life. He had reason to do so. The emperor Frederick Barbarossa was Otto's nephew. On succeeding to the empire in 1152, Frederick planned to restore his Reich to its former glory. Propaganda played an important part in his campaign; he would publicize the glorious past of the empire in histories. Otto received a request from his nephew to send a copy of the *History of the Two Cities*. He complied with misgivings. Its account of the decline and ruin of the empire would not suit Frederick's purpose at all. The bishop of Freising excused himself for his pessimism. He wrote a preface to explain that he had written the *History* in dismal times. He also asked Rainald of Dassel, Frederick's chancellor and adviser on the propaganda campaign, to interpret the *History* to Frederick in such a way that it would not displease him. The emperor reassured the author: he had read the book and enjoyed it; but he decided to employ Otto's talents to advertise his achievements in restoring the empire. Otto was put into the position of a doctor who has diagnosed a mortal illness and then has to celebrate his patient's recovery. He set about it with a good heart.

The new book belonged to a different genre, as its title shows: *The Deeds of Frederick*. This genre made periodization unnecessary. Otto could concentrate on the illustrious story of Frederick's family and on his prowess as a young man. Then he reaches Frederick's accession. Clear morning has followed a dark, rainy night. Otto rewrites the history of the empire from the conflict between Henry IV and Gregory VII up to Frederick's accession, giving it a new slant; he brings out the rise of Frederick's family while toning down Henry IV's reverses and the decline of the empire. He tells of Frederick's successes in glowing terms. The new ruler was a righteous man; he restored the empire and worked in harmony with the Church, as his forbears had done in the good old days before the Investiture Conflict. Otto's praise must have been sincere. Frederick's early achievements in Germany and Italy could not have failed to gratify a kinsman and bishop of the imperial Church. How far did they lead him to revise his view of the pattern of universal history? We do not know. Otto continued to take an interest in events outside the empire. He exceeded his instructions by making digressions (fortunately for the value of his *Deeds*) and sometimes excused himself for not keeping to his subject. But he did not try to fit his material into the time schemes of the *Two Cities*. Empire, like religion, had upset the timetable by taking on a new lease of life. Otto contented himself with warning Frederick to beware of Fortune's Wheel. Perhaps he

51 The emperor Frederick Barbarossa sits beside Bishop Albert of Freising, the successor of Otto of Freising. From a jamb of the door of Freising cathedral, about 1200.

thought that the revival might not last. Perhaps he also admitted that his pattern of history needed revision. If so, he kept his view to himself; it is still a secret.

The Deeds of Frederick breaks off unfinished at Otto's death in 1158. He had asked his chaplain, Rahewin, to continue the book. Rahewin carried it down to 1160. His continuation shows that he was a good craftsman and a sound historian; but the genre did not call for reflective history.

His restraint symbolizes the future of medieval historiography. Otto's successors focused increasingly on the present, without questioning its relevance to the old time schemes.

Civil-service history

The term 'civil service' today evokes a picture of conventional men in secure jobs. A civil service existed in the twelfth century; but it was a new development in medieval government. Bureaucrats were not yet smothered by routine. In his great book on feudal society Marc Bloch argues that the rise of the salaried worker or employee marked a new stage in medieval history. The number of clerks staffing embryonic bureaucracies increased, and these 'black-coated workers' began to divide themselves into what we now call the 'administrative' and 'executive' grades of the civil service. Some worked their way up to the higher grade and got to the top, while others stayed in the lower ranks until they retired. Their employers were royal, municipal and ecclesiastical governments; all needed accountants and administrators. We have seen that William of St Thierry counted 'varieties of positions and posts' in his list of novelties perceptible in his time. The civil service offered just such a choice of career to young men in search of a livelihood, provided that they had a basic training in 'the three Rs'.

Some bureaucrats wrote history in their spare time or had leisure thrust upon them, which they used to draw up their memoirs. We might expect a civil-service historian to write in a different style from a monk. He did indeed. He had a different outlook and more direct experience. His work would often involve him in riots and other disturbances; he did not lead the sheltered life of the cloister. Our first specimen of civil-service history has the title *The Murder of Charles the Good*.

This is a precious freak of historiography. The author, Galbert of Bruges, worked as a notary for the chapter of the cathedral in his native town. He belonged to the 'executive' grade, being a clerk in minor orders, unbeneficed, as far as we know, and probably living on his perquisites and fees. The occasion for his writing was the murder in 1127 of Count Charles of Flanders while he knelt in the cathedral at prayer. His assassins were members of the powerful Erlembald

52 Opposite: civil servants. Muslim and Latin notaries at work at the royal court at Palermo. A detail from an illustration to Peter of Eboli's poem celebrating the conquest of Sicily by the emperor Henry VI in 1195 (see also colour plate II). *Bern, Burgerbibliothek, Cod. 120, f.101r*

family of servile stock. Count Charles had planned to investigate their origins and perhaps reduce them to serfdom once more. They took desperate measures to save themselves. After the murder the clan occupied the castle of Bruges, adjacent to the cathedral, and carried war into the countryside. It spread over the whole county of Flanders. Galbert must have had time on his hands, since the rebels moved the chapter archives into the castle. His normal business as a notary ceased. He resolved to keep a day-to-day record of the dreadful happenings around him. The task kept him going, and he felt a sort of compulsion, 'a little spark of charity', as he calls it. We miss the tired old excuse of writing to order. Galbert wrote on his own initiative, freshly and precisely; he had the legal precision of his calling.

Since the murdered count had no heir, a claimant to the county came forward in the person of William Clito, who was backed by the king of France. The rebels had first to be dislodged from the castle, since its possession carried control over the town. The burghers of Bruges and of the neighbouring town of Ghent snatched at the opportunity to wring concessions from their new lord. They clubbed together and sold their help for promises. It was a new and clever step towards winning their freedom from burdens imposed by their lord. Clito made promises at the expense of the count's vassals, whose rights to levy taxes he abolished. The burghers of Bruges and Ghent helped him to defeat the rebels after a fearsome struggle, only to rebel in their turn when he failed to honour his agreement: he had dipped his hands into other men's pockets. Clito's expulsion from Flanders brought more wars, as other claimants to the county (there were four in all) tried their luck at conquest. Galbert followed the complicated chain of events down to the restoration of peace. Then he added an introduction and some chapters of explanation to make the origins of the dispute clearer.

Galbert addressed himself to the men of Bruges and to 'all the faithful'. He had a sense of solidarity with his fellow townsmen, in spite of their misbehaviour, which he was the first to recognize. He blames the king of France, the nobles, clergy and burghers impartially; all committed crimes and blunders. He could see both sides of the question. The murderers of Count Charles were guilty of treason, and sacrilege too, and deserved their fate. On the other hand, it was natural for them to fight against the prospect of losing their status. Galbert's receptive mind saved him from being cocksure about the workings of Providence. At first he saw the troubles as God's punishment for treason against one's lord, which is forbidden in Scripture. Then the story became more complex; he admitted to being puzzled. His observation was unclouded by learning. Suetonius contributed nothing to the notary's shrewd, vivid character sketches. Galbert rose to his opportunity and innovated.

Galbert's murder story is unique. My next example, the *Annals of Genoa*, is chosen as the first of a long line of city annals and chronicles. Genoa differed from Bruges in as much as the Flemish towns owed their growing prosperity to textiles; the burghers had to safeguard their profits against their lords' efforts to hive them off by exacting dues and supervising the town government. Genoese prosperity depended on seaborne trade. The citizens turned to the sea because a mountainous hinterland hemmed them in. Genoese merchants enriched themselves by trade, by naval war against the Saracens and by piracy. A few wealthy families managed the city. The emperor was their legal overlord; but he lacked the means to interfere with them. They pushed their bishop into the background; he became a help rather than a hindrance. Business techniques in the form of accounting, investment-sharing, and insurance to offset the dangers of seafaring, developed early. Hence literacy was a 'must' for the merchants and their office workers.

The city government also called for literacy. Merchants of the wealthier families served as consuls and went on embassies to foreign powers. Caffaro, the first Genoese annalist, was a literate layman who belonged to a ruling family; he was born into the 'administrative' grade. He took part in politics and in battles too. His editor compares him to Julius Caesar: he made history as well as writing it. At the age of twenty he went on crusade with the Genoese expedition to Palestine, where he fought in sieges and visited the holy places. His *Annals* begin in 1099, a conscious choice, since the year opened a new stage in the city's history: the first communal government was formed and an unprecedented large-scale naval expedition set out. Caffaro presented his *Annals*, kept up to date, to the consuls and council of Genoa in 1152. They ordered his book to be copied at public cost: it should tell the Genoese of their city's victories for all time. He continued his record up to his eightieth year, and died in 1166.

This layman's record is written in clear, correct Latin without frills. The annalist does not efface himself. He

mentions his own experience and the fact that he had access to the city archives, while keeping a discreet silence on state secrets. Where there is no need for secrecy, he gives precise details of city finances, of the measurements of buildings and of the number of galleys dispatched on forays. He makes first-hand reports on imperial and papal councils. His aim was to glorify Genoa and he admits to passing over her slacker periods briefly. It is the spirit of the parish pump; but the Genoese parish stretched over the whole Mediterranean. His ideas on politics show the practical outlook of the Italian city-states. He handles the conflict between pope and emperor in a masterly way. Genoa gained from both sides. Frederick I needed money for his Italian campaigns; he put city privileges up for sale. The Genoese received special imperial privileges, though Caffaro lets out the fact that they paid through the nose. Pope Alexander III stayed at Genoa when his quarrel with Frederick forced him to escape to France. The port was his escape route, so he paid special honour to the citizens. Caffaro wrote that the devil had stirred up discord in the Church, and left it at that. He did not state what he must have known, that from the papal point of view Frederick was an excommunicate and schismatic when he granted privileges to Genoa. Why take sides when you could batten on both? Genoa's real enemies were the Pisans, her trading rivals. Caffaro hated them much more than the Saracens, whose sea power had declined. Enemies nearer home were the country nobles, a danger to peace and naturally hostile to a mercantile commune. He had no reason to be anti-clerical; the clergy's teeth had been drawn; but his lay mind shows through when he tells of a dangerous outbreak of fire in Genoa. A monastic chronicler would have credited its control and extinction to the miraculous power of the local saints. Caffaro praises the citizens for putting it out by their own efforts.

Galbert and Caffaro have one thing in common, their *esprit de corps*. Both identify themselves with their city, Galbert during the bloodshed and misery at Bruges, Caffaro with Genoa during her brilliant rise to power. To Galbert, Bruges was 'my city right or wrong': he did recognize standards of right and wrong. Caffaro felt that they hardly came into it when Genoese interests were involved.

John of Salisbury brings us back to learned clerical circles. He was an academic ecclesiastical administrator. His long years of study in France enabled him to meet the best masters of his time. In 1147 he joined the household of Archbishop Theobald of Canterbury. John proved himself to be a skilled letter-writer and rose to be Theobald's private secretary. He has been described as a failed academic. Perhaps he would have preferred to teach in the schools, had he succeeded in finding a chair and the wherewithal to finance himself. But his duties as secretary allowed him leisure to read and write and money to buy books, though never enough to satisfy him. He also went on diplomatic business abroad, where he met former masters and fellow-students. He mixed freely with princes, prelates and popes.

Only one of John's many writings is historical in the strict sense of the word. He called it *Historia pontificalis*, which has been aptly translated as *Memoirs of the Papal Court*. John's ambition was to write ecclesiastical history after the manner of Eusebius. He read the histories available and found that none went down any further than the end of the Council of Rheims in 1148. He therefore started with the council, giving a fuller account of it than his source; he had attended it in person with his archbishop. He chose to focus his history on the papal court. It was a rational way to organize a history of the Church in the mid-twelfth century, when the Curia was becoming a centre of government for the whole of Latin Christendom. All roads led to Rome or to

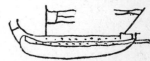

54, 55 Marginal illustrations to Caffaro's *Annals of Genoa*. Top: a butcher chopping up meat points to the record of a law which ordered slaughterhouses to be moved outside the city in the interests of hygiene. Above: a Genoese galley points to a naval expedition.

111

56 A Cistercian abbot, probably St Bernard of Clairvaux, is shown on the west front of the twelfth-century church of Our Lady at Maastricht.

wherever the pope might be. John was able to make digressions on Church matters in other countries in connection with appeals to Rome and so on. His *Memoirs*, as we have them, break off in 1152. He probably wrote them up from his notes in 1164. He had kept his post on the archiepiscopal staff after Theobald's death; then the quarrel between Becket and Henry II forced him to take refuge in France. His exile gave him further opportunities for writing.

The *Historia pontificalis* is the memoirs of a scholar-diplomat, who recalls his experiences and whose highly-placed friends kept him primed with news. It is free from cant and rhetoric. The speeches recorded there sound like verbatim reports from memory or from notes taken soon afterwards. John's urbane cattiness makes him good reading. He criticizes almost everyone, except his patron Theobald, and loves to report witty sayings. He had his prejudices; what diplomat has not? John was pro-French and anti-German. A churchman of blameless life, writing for a likeminded friend, Abbot Peter of la Celle, he felt free to judge the pope and cardinals severely. The visit of two papal legates to Germany gave him a welcome opportunity to score off both the legates and the Germans. However, he tried hard to be fair. His account of the Council of Rheims brought all his qualities of fairness and tact into play. It is justly famous as a scrupulous effort to present both sides of a dispute. John describes the trial of Gilbert of la Porrée, his former master, now bishop of Poitiers, on a charge of heresy sponsored by St Bernard of Clairvaux. John admired Gilbert as a man and as a scholar. He venerated St Bernard as a saint. Bernard, moreover, had written John a testimonial, without ever having set eyes on him, when John had left the schools and was looking for a post. He had personal obligations to the abbot of Clairvaux, who showed his trust in him by sending him as a messenger to Gilbert after the trial. Bernard regarded Gilbert as a dangerous teacher of error; to Gilbert, Bernard was an interfering amateur in academic questions. John does his best for them. He clears them both on the score of good intentions, sympathizing with Gilbert as an intellectual, but respecting Bernard's motives as 'zeal for God's house'. He gives a careful account of procedure at the trial, as he remembered it, and of the heresies imputed to Gilbert. Backstairs intrigue and self-interest held no secrets from him. Memoirs are always more readable when we know some of the people in the story. John's important friends and acquaintances appear in other contemporary sources, but nowhere else do they come to life so clearly.

So far our civil-servant historians have worked for municipal or ecclesiastical governments. In England, the reign of Henry II (1154–89) saw the rise of something more like a modern government machine. Henry's staff were royal servants first and foremost; but the better educated among them already had the idea that they were public servants too. Henry put new content into the ancient Roman tradition of rule. A Roman emperor wielded public power for the public good, *utilitas reipublicae*. The private interest of subjects should give way to the good of the commonwealth. Early medieval histories of rulers tended to present the king as a war-leader; churchmen normally judged him according to his record as protector of the Church. Yet the ancient notion that 'public power' was vested in the ruler was never forgotten. It lies behind Richer's false statement that Hugh Capet 'established laws and made decrees'. Richer adjusted the actions of the king to his ideas of what a ruler ought to do.

Henry II really did hold assizes, which issued administrative and judicial ordinances. He also reformed judicial procedure. His reforms had a dual purpose. They brought money to his treasury and they tightened his grip on his kingdom; at the same time they benefited free landholders by providing quicker and fairer modes of legal action. Litigants (and every landholder was a litigant in the Middle Ages) took advantage of Henry's reforms. The king showed a personal interest in improving his government. He surrounded himself with legal experts and hammered out his projects with their advice.

Civil servants have a vested interest in the establishment. Henry's men could also feel proud of it, admiring his reforms and sharing in the credit of devising and supervising the new methods. Technical treatises on government were written such as the *Dialogue of the Exchequer* and *On the Laws of England*. A good example of history as written by a retired civil servant is the *Chronicle* of Roger of Howden.

Roger took his name from his parsonage of Howden in Yorkshire. He had the title of 'Master': degrees were becoming a passport to civil service posts. He entered Henry's employment in about 1174. His work gave him an opportunity to observe the seamy as well as the more likeable side of Angevin bureaucracy. Roger served as

Justice of the Forest almost continuously between 1185 and 1190. These justices went round the country holding Courts of the Forest and fining people for poaching and other offences against forest law. Enforcement of the forest laws was the most oppressive and unpopular aspect of Angevin rule. Roger retired from service in order to go on the Third Crusade in company with a small group of northerners. On returning home in 1191, he settled down at Howden to write his book, and died in 1201/2.

The book is called a 'chronicle'. Its author did not intend to write a history with literary flourishes and analysis of causes. The chief interest of the chronicle is that Roger gave so much space to his record of government measures. He copied documents as evidence and illustrated the details of administration from his inside knowledge. This was a new type of documentation. Eusebius had inserted documents in order to prove how the Church had triumphed over her persecutors and won recognition. Monastic historiographers did the same in the interests of their community. Bruno documented his *Saxon War* in order to vindicate the Saxons. Roger of Howden wanted to hold Henry II up to admiration as a reformer; but there is also a note of sheer pleasure in his description of how royal government worked. He respected Henry's energy in devising reforms and noted his care for justice: on one occasion the king reversed a decision made by his Chief Justice because he knew that the latter had a personal grudge against the litigant. Roger took a shrewd look at foreign affairs. He understood the role of finance: Prince John's expedition to Ireland failed for the reason that John was too tight-fisted to pay his mercenaries their wages. To read through the chronicle is to see that Roger had the defects of his merits. He does not stop to reflect as he writes. Inconsistency did not bother him. His mind was a rag-bag. He veered from one side to another when he narrated a dispute; he was both pro-Henry and pro-Becket. His only constant principles or prejudices were dislike of archbishops and papal legates on the one hand, and loyalty to Henry II against rebels and foreign enemies on the other. He had the limitations of a 'second-grade administrator'.

Master Ralph of Diss in Norfolk was a grander person than Roger of Howden and more of an intellectual. He studied both Arts and theology and perhaps also taught at Paris. He made his career in the cathedral church of St Paul in London, where he held various offices and rose to the position of dean in about 1180. He functioned as dean until his death in 1202. Ralph counts as a 'supply civil servant and diplomat'; the Angevin kings employed him on commissions and embassies as a valued expert on legal and administrative matters. His office as dean, in charge of the chapter estates and head of the chapter of St Paul's, made him an administrator in his own right. He was a successful estate-manager and a realistic, sensible reformer of the chapter. The canons remembered him as 'the good dean'. Ralph's historical works consist of a short world chronicle, the *Abridgment of Chronicles*, going down to 1147, and a bigger book, *Pictures* or *Reflections of Histories*. This begins with the knighting of the future King Henry II in 1148 and continues until the writer's death. He prepared for it by collecting a large dossier over many years. The first draft was ready by 1190. The *Pictures of Histories* is written in annalistic form. It focuses on England, but includes notices on foreign affairs. Ralph brings himself into it, when he had taken part in the events he recorded. He was too important a person to need to obtrude himself. If he had a weakness, it was to copy in letters of advice which he had written to his friends. But then his advice had been asked for. One consulted the dean as a man whose head was screwed firmly on his shoulders.

The concept of 'public power' inspired his account of royal government. Roger of Howden described its practice; Ralph linked practice to theory. Warmly approving of its development, he copied Henry II's assizes, records of tax collection, forest laws and so on into his annals. They all go to show how Henry used his public power to benefit the commonwealth. There was no public power in Ireland to keep the peace before Henry's invasion. Public power must override private interests; Henry saw that it should. To quote a classic passage under the year 1179:

The king sought to help those of his subjects who could least help themselves, having found that the sheriffs were using the public power in their own private interests. Hence the king, in his growing anxiety for the public welfare, entrusted rights of justice to other loyal men of his realm, so that representatives of the public power should terrify delinquents when they toured the provinces . . . and that those guilty of offences against the royal majesty should incur royal anger.

Ralph goes on to specify Henry's measures to curb the power of the sheriffs in local government by sending round royal justices. He underlines Henry's care for justice throughout his kingdom and his experiments in controlling his agents. He hoped that Henry would use his public power in order to protect the weak against the strong. How far Henry actually did so is another matter. Of the three kings who come into the *Pictures*, Ralph prefers Henry, because he showed most skill in government. Richard I ranks lower, in spite of his military exploits. John had already blotted his copy-book by rebelling against his father and elder brother while still a prince.

The concept of public power, wielded for the public good, can lead on to that of the nation state. It is interesting to see whether Ralph of Diss made the step from one concept to the other or whether he had any notion of England as a nation. When Ralph describes a rebellion he stresses filial piety and loyalty to one's lord as his touchstone of conduct. He does not blame rebels as traitors to their country. His affection centred on the reigning house of Anjou rather than on England, which was only part of their dominions. He could hardly have subscribed to the xenophobic saying ascribed to an Englishman of the nineteenth century: 'Niggers begin at Calais'. Henry II and his sons would have been 'niggers' in that case. They came of mixed parentage, Norman, Angevin and French; their territories in France stretched from the Channel to the Pyrenees. Ralph, however, was prejudiced against the peoples outside France. Over her borders the uncivilized races begin: the Saxons are stony-hearted; the Austrians have dirty habits; Sicily produces tyrants. Some form of xenophobia began before what we call 'national feeling' had impinged on historiography.

A second question arises: how did Ralph's view of royal power as public power affect his presentation of the conflict between his king and his archbishop? Henry's quarrel with Thomas Becket brought up the problem of the relations between the 'two powers' of medieval political theory, *regnum* and *sacerdotium*, monarchy and clergy. As dean of St Paul's, Ralph lived through the conflict with credit, keeping in with both sides. Though Ralph stayed in England and remained on excellent terms with Henry and with Gilbert Foliot, Becket's chief opponent among the bishops, the exiled archbishop and his circle regarded him as a friend; he never incurred the reproach of being disloyal to the Church. To steer his way through the conflict was easier than to narrate it without committing himself. Ralph worked for two establishments, the Church and the Crown. They collaborated below the surface all the time; but they clashed openly some of the time. Then as now, conflict had more news value than harmony. Ralph was in a difficulty. He could not omit the events which led up to Becket's murder. The martyr was now a canonized saint: Ralph could not blame St Thomas for dying in defence of the liberties of the Church in England. On the other hand, an admirer of Henry's government could not approve of Becket's attempts at sabotage, for that was what they seemed to be.

To begin with a minor point at issue: canon law forbad churchmen to hold secular office. The reasons were moral and legal. Ecclesiastics who had cure of souls should devote themselves to their pastoral care. Legally they were forbidden to take part in any function which involved bloodshed: secular jurisdiction involved passing sentence of death or mutilation on persons convicted of felony. Still less should a churchman have custody of a castle or lead a military expedition. Yet kings rewarded their clerks with bishoprics, as a means of financing royal government out of Church revenues and feeding talent into the royal administration. The canon law ruling, if strictly enforced, would have caused a brain-drain from the civil service. Ralph saw the civil service as instituted for the public good; yet its practice went against canon law. His writings show that he wobbled on the question of principle. On the whole he thought that a bishop was justified in holding secular office, provided that he had permission from his ecclesiastical superiors. That was reasonable, since the ban could be relaxed and was enforced only occasionally.

The minor issue leads on to the major. Becket insisted on obeying the letter of canon law. On becoming archbishop, he renounced his office as royal chancellor. Then came his clash with Henry on the question of clerical privilege and ecclesiastical liberties in general, followed by his exile and murder. His shrine at Canterbury attracted pilgrims from all over Christendom.

The heroic way to present the conflict would have been to use shades of grey instead of black and white. Ralph might have taken the line that each side in the conflict was 'partly right and partly wrong'. That would have been a taxing assignment for a contemporary writer and would probably have given offence all round. Yet Ralph was more thoughtful than Roger of Howden, who slapped down incompatible

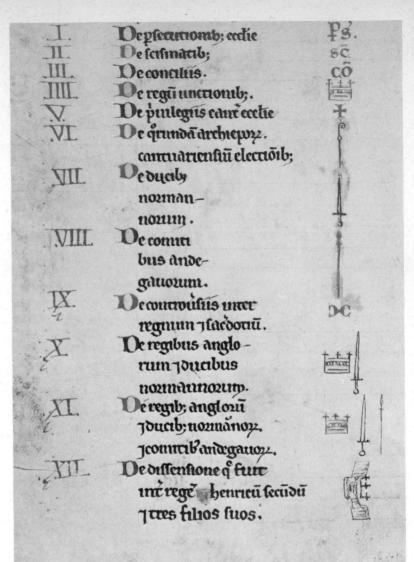

57 A page from the copy of his historical works presented by Ralph of Diss to St Paul's, showing signs which he used to classify the subject matter in his histories. The crown, for instance, indicates matter 'on the anointing of kings', the long sword refers to the dukes of Normandy, and the symbol at the bottom, in which two hands grasp a crown, denotes the conflict between Henry II and his sons. *London, Lambeth Palace Library, MS 8, f.1r*

opinions without comment. The dean could not bring himself to be so inconsistent. He found a way out of the *impasse* by inventing a system of pigeon-holing.

His material is divided into parallel columns. One column contains what we now call 'political' history, that is, the deeds of kings. Another contains records of battles, and another ecclesiastical history – the successions of popes and bishops and church councils. Ralph allocated yet another column to conflict between secular and ecclesiastical powers. He devised special signs to put in the margin to distinguish each notice. A battle, for instance, is marked by crossed swords. He explains his method in his introduction and uses it both in his *Abridgment of Chronicles* and in his *Pictures of Histories*. The advantage of his arrangement was that juxtaposition made synthesis and judgment unnecessary. Each event could be recorded in its place. Conflicts could be narrated without prejudice to the protagonists.

Earlier historiographers had used parallel columns in order to synchronize pagan and Christian history. Ralph went further and synchronized the events of Christian history, keeping its different aspects separate from one another. He may have had other precedents for his method, but they have not survived. There may be a clue in the scrapbook of excerpts from earlier writers which Ralph had copied as a preface to his historical books. An example given by Hugh of St Victor appealed to him, and he included it in his scrapbook. Hugh advises students to keep the diverse kinds of wisdom separate. You waste your time and addle your brain if you mix them. He instances the money-changers of Paris, who keep their diverse kinds of coinage in purses divided into compartments. These handy contraptions enable them to change currency so quickly and easily that the people standing round them gape and wonder to see so many sorts of coinage coming out of the same wallet. The example must have amused Ralph; he was a financial expert himself. Perhaps he pondered Hugh's tip to students on keeping their files in order and adapted it to historical presentation.

Ralph of Diss certainly anticipates a good deal of modern historiography. Much of it has turned into a vast system of pigeon-holing. We keep our data in separate compartments; the method is time-saving and thought-saving. It has its uses as a preliminary; but we abuse the method if we make it an end in itself. We need not imitate Ralph, but we can sympathize with his dilemma and his search for a solution.

9
Conquest and crusade

Most people today feel uneasy about the crusades and see them as an unpleasing feature of medieval history. We have had enough of wars and especially of so-called ideological wars. The crusaders were blood-thirsty fanatics. Worse than that, some of them were 'on the make'; they used the holy wars to make unholy gains. We have to stretch our historical imagination to understand their mentality.

Another less healthy prejudice against the crusaders springs from our tendency to judge a movement by its success. The crusading movement can be written off as a failure, doomed from the start. It is a sorry record: the Latins failed to establish a permanent kingdom in Palestine; Saladin captured Jerusalem in 1187; the Latin kingdom dwindled to a coastal strip; the last stronghold at Acre fell in 1291. The Fourth Crusade of 1204 was diverted from its purpose to capture the Christian city of Constantinople. The Latin kingdom established on the site of the former Byzantine empire had disappeared by 1260. Our prejudice against the crusades as failures will weaken, however, if we think of the expeditions to Palestine as only the most far-flung of many campaigns which aimed to enlarge the bounds of Christendom. Some of these campaigns were very successful indeed. Spain was reconquered from the Moors by a joint effort: French knights crossed the Pyrenees to help the Spanish Christians and settled in the peninsula. On the eastern frontier of Germany the pagan Slavs between the Elbe and the Oder were conquered and converted.

Crusades were launched for objects other than wars against the infidel. The popes turned them against heretics too. Crusaders from northern France came south to fight against the Albigensian heretics. They also succeeded in defeating the southern nobles. The Capetian kings followed in their wake and took over the Midi. The partial Anglo-Norman conquest of Ireland could be presented as a kind of crusade, though here its victims were 'backward' Catholics, not heretics.

58 A warrior against evil. Detail of a capital on the porch of the church at Rebolledo de la Torre, in Castile, early thirteenth-century.

59 Relations between German colonists and Slavs are described in the *Sachsenspiegel*, the oldest German law-book. This illustration and the one opposite (ill. 60) come from a copy produced about 1320. Here, lords who receive enfeoffment of lands east of the river Saal in Prussia are obliged to take part in campaigns against the heathen Slavs on their borders. *Heidelberg, Universitätsbibliothek, Cod. Pal. Germ. 164, f.1v*

All these campaigns secured permanent results: they all left their mark on the map of Europe. Contemporaries could not have foreseen that the Latins would fail on one front only, in Palestine. The amazing victories of the First Crusade naturally led to the expectation that 'France Overseas' had come to stay. We have to share this confidence when we read medieval histories of the crusades.

Conquest and crusade had a liberating and stimulating effect on historiography. The novelty and excitement of the story freed its historians from dependence on ancient models. There was nothing comparable in ancient and early medieval history; the historian of the crusades had to express himself in his own way. Writing became less mannered and more spontaneous. Widening horizons gave stimulus. Historians living in a military zone had a new experience; they observed two cultures. Since the wars were intermittent and long-drawn-out, settlers in conquered territory had peaceful contacts with the enemy: it is always an eye-opener to discover that one's enemies are people and not devils.

Defeat supplied an even stronger stimulus than victory. It led to heart-searching. Saracen penetration of Palestine, the slow pace of conquest and conversion on the German border, the standstill of the Anglo-Norman venture in Ireland, all raised the question why God deserted his servants when they were fighting in his cause. Why did he delay or withhold success from the faithful? The spread of heresies within the body of Christendom, especially in the Midi, made some historians wonder who was responsible. Earlier writers had sometimes refrained from criticizing contemporaries for

60 German colonists in eastern Europe clear waste-land and build a village. An illustration from the *Sachsenspiegel* (see ill. 59, opposite). *Heidelberg, Universitätsbibliothek, Cod. Pal. Germ. 164, f.26v*

fear of offending them. Historians of the crusades were more daring, perhaps because authority functioned more weakly in a border area.

The crusades produced lay authors and vernacular histories. A laymen's literature developed. The new type of history contrasted with traditional Latin ecclesiastical historiography in many respects. At the same time, it was far removed from the vernacular epic or *chanson de geste*. These dealt mainly with fiction; a crusading history would start from facts.

The stories of 'conquest historians' are less dramatic and exotic than the crusaders', but they will help us to understand the crusading mentality. The German conquest of the Slavs will make a good starting-point. Master Adam of Bremen wrote the *Deeds of the Archbishops of Bremen* in the late eleventh century. He used the traditional genre of the history of an episcopal see as a frame for a wider story: this border city was a centre for the conquest and conversion of the heathen Slavs across the frontier. Adam inserted a geo-graphical account of 'all Slavia', which he calls 'a very large province of Germany'. Medieval accounts of unknown territory normally included legends and marvels. Adam makes no exception to the rule; 'marvels of the East' such as Cyclops and Amazons come into his description; but he was scientific enough to add reports collected by himself and his own observations on the peoples and their countries. The Slav gods or 'idols' interested him. It was more than mere curiosity about the unfamiliar. He could see the point of view of the Slav victims of German expansion. True, he tells atrocity stories of the massacre of Christian priests, but he

does not shrink from exposing the misdeeds of Christians. Members of a newly founded mission church in Slav territory took to robbery; naturally, Adam tells us, they provoked reprisals from the Slavs.

His position in a border city sharpened his political insight: he describes a three-cornered conflict between the Slavs, the princes and the bishops. Each group had its own motives. The Slavs resisted the Germans; the bishops wanted to convert them, partly because their conversion would increase the power and wealth of the Church; the princes cared only to conquer them. If the Slavs were converted, then the princes had to share the fruits of conquest with the bishops, since bishops had a right to take tithes from Christians. Adam felt that blame for the slow pace of conversion fell on princes and prelates alike. He makes a king of Denmark say that all the Slavs could have been converted long ago, but for the greed of the Saxons in making them pay tribute when they became subjects.

The history of a see gave its writer opportunities to portray the characters of the bishops. The archbishops of Hamburg–Bremen ruled over an expanding border area; the region

61, 62 Tenth-century missionary work. Opposite: St Adalbert of Prague baptizes Prussian converts. Left: his head and body are exposed after his martyrdom by the heathen. Details from the bronze doors of Gniezno cathedral, about 1170.

offered dazzling prospects to an ambitious prelate. He could enlarge his boundaries and make himself an indispensable ally in German politics. Adam had a challenging sitter for a portrait in Archbishop Adalbert (d. 1071). He made full use of it, breathing new life into the tradition of character description. At last we have a moving picture instead of a 'still'. Adalbert's ambition turned into megalomania. Adam writes as an almost clinical observer of the onset of symptoms. He shows us the interplay of character and circumstances. The various strands in the archbishop's character are linked to his victories and reverses. Its inner unity comes through as well as the process of his *folie de grandeur*. Adam has traced an unforgettable story of a person. He might easily have looked at his subject as a moralist and resorted to the theme of Fortune's Wheel. Instead he innovated. Perhaps his unusual environment influenced him to set down his experience as an observer.

Helmold, priest of Bosau, owed much of his inspiration to Adam, though he wrote almost a century later and described the conquest at a later stage. He had read the *Deeds*, which provided him with a precedent and a source for the early history of the Slavs. Helmold's book is called the *Chronicle of the Slavs*; but the title is posthumous. The book is really a glorification of Christian missions to the heathen. Praise of the missionaries leads on to the history of military campaigns and to the rise of cities in conquered lands. Helmold dedicated his book to the canons of Lübeck, his mother church. His patron, Bishop Gerold, had advised him that this would be the best way to honour Lübeck. The first part of the *Chronicle of the Slavs* was finished in 1167/8, the second part in 1172. Adam's account of Archbishop Adalbert shows us a changing character; Helmold's book shows us a developing historian. The change in his attitude to his material is one of the most interesting features of his *Chronicle*. Like Adam, he wrote from first-hand experience; he had worked in the mission field; but his observation led him to see his story differently as it unfolded.

At first he used Adam's *Deeds*, making alterations which point to a more critical and worldly outlook. He suppressed the 'marvels' and checked Adam's ecclesiastical bias by giving more credit to the princes than the prelates in the work of conquest and conversion. He improved on his source by including archaeological evidence for the early stages: ruined churches and dykes in Slav territories bore witness to the tenth-century occupation by the Saxons, before the Slav reaction drove them back. He reminds us of Bede's use of surviving Roman remains as evidence for the Roman occupation of Britain.

The three-cornered conflict of interests described by Adam persisted in Helmold's day, and he was just as aware of it. The princes had no interest in converting the Slavs. They did not warm to the idea of the crusade against the Slavs preached by St Bernard in 1146 at the same time as he preached the Second Crusade to the Holy Land. The Slavs, according to St Bernard, were to be either 'converted or else wholly destroyed'. If 'wholly destroyed', they would not have been able to pay tribute to their conquerors. The hero of Helmold's story is his patron, Bishop Vicelin. This bishop was a true missionary; Helmold admired him. Then, after Vicelin's death, Henry the Lion, duke of Saxony, steps into his place as the leader of eastward expansion. The change of leadership marks a change in Helmold's outlook. He began to think better of armed force. Duke Henry was both heroic and greedy. At first 'he cared nothing for Christianity', in Helmold's words, 'but only for money'. Later, Henry could afford the luxury of supporting mission work, provided that he kept a tight hand on the missionaries. He was rich and successful enough as a conqueror and colonizer to go shares with the Church in exploiting the defeated peoples. Henry treated his clergy as his servants. Helmold judged that submission to the ducal will was not too high a price to pay for freedom to evangelize. He approved of those churchmen who obeyed the duke, even though it meant waiving ecclesiastical liberties.

Helmold resembled Adam in his curiosity about the Slavs. His *Chronicle* has a wider scope than the *Deeds*, in that it tells the story of three peoples, the Saxons, the Danes, who took part in the conquest, and the Slavs of the area. He portrays the virtues and vices peculiar to each people, not sparing the Saxons or the Danes. In describing the Slavs he notes what struck him as good in their customs and values: their hospitality to friends and strangers alike impressed him, though he adds that they would steal in order to find the wherewithal to feed their guests. He records the various religious observances of their tribes. Of course, he lacked a social anthropologist's understanding of their beliefs, which were primitive by his standards; but he realized that tribal customs were not uniform. Given a colonist's prejudice against the 'natives', it is surprising that he described them so objectively. He had a real sympathy for their dilemma as the conquerors' grip on them tightened; the Slavs could not escape by land or by sea. They were surrounded by enemies and had no resources left.

Helmold's sympathy for the conquered diminished as he began to rejoice at the effects of the conquest. Henry the Lion brought prosperity to his duchy by attracting settlers from foreign lands and by founding cities. The fortified port of Lübeck grew into a rich trading emporium. To Helmold it was a beautiful sight. The new prosperity delighted him. The Old Testament rears its head at this point. The conquerors resembled the children of Israel, expelling the gentiles from the Promised Land. The Slav lands between the Elbe and the Oder, if not yet flowing with milk and honey, could be made to. Settlers were clearing and draining the waste and turning it into farmland. Helmold lost interest in the fate of the Slavs. Economically, the settlers had replaced them. The natives were almost wiped out; those who escaped destruction were subjected to strict discipline. Slav vagrants were to be caught and hanged. The book ends on this colonial note, at variance with Helmold's earlier enthusiasm for mission work.

The *Chronicle* portrays individuals as well as peoples. Helmold was a student of character. He had no such giant as Archbishop Adalbert to stretch his powers; but he did his best with what was available. Bishops Gerold and Vicelin appear as the conventional type of 'the good prelate', as they may in fact have been. Gerold's successor as bishop did not fit into any type. Helmold presents him as a human mixture of good and bad qualities. Henry the Lion had foisted him on the chapter of Lübeck against the canons' wishes. Troubles followed; the Lion's protégé suffered from the canons' hostility. Helmold shows him changing, in the opposite direction to Adalbert: exile and sorrow taught him compassion for his fellow-men. Again we can enjoy a moving picture instead of a mere catalogue of personal characteristics. Secular princes are sketched in the course of the story, with their varying degrees of prowess and miscreancy. Helmold quotes the cliché that truth will offend, but only to flout the consequences: 'Blame yourself and not the mirror if you don't like what you see there.' His mirror must have shown some red faces. He became ruthless in his attitude to the natives; but he was equally so in describing their conquerors; no holds are barred.

The Anglo-Norman conquest of Ireland found a historian in Giraldus Cambrensis, or Gerald of Wales (d. 1220). Gerald was no local man, like Adam and Helmold. He was a scholar of international fame, well educated in rhetoric, law and theology. But he had local connections. He was descended from a Welsh royal house on his mother's side; his father belonged to a family of Norman Marcher lords, settled in South Wales; his relatives won estates in Ireland. Gerald was a brilliant observer, entertainer and satirist. His satire was sharpened by the failure of his ambition: he wanted to become bishop of St David's and to have the see raised to the status of archbishopric. In spite of pressure on the Angevin kings and repeated visits to the papal court, he rose to be archdeacon of St David's and no further.

Two trips to Ireland, lasting about a year each, enabled Gerald to collect material for two books, *On the Topography of Ireland* and *On the Conquest of Ireland*. The first is descriptive; the second brings the first up to date by narrating the attempted conquest of Ireland; it ends after Prince John's expedition of 1185. Gerald had accompanied the prince on the orders of John's father, Henry II. The *Conquest* was dedicated to the future King Richard I. It stands on the borderline between two types of history. It is a historical monograph, written in Latin; but Gerald felt the pull of a wider audience. He hoped that someone would translate the *Conquest* into French. He wrote in what he calls a plain modern style: his Muse jibbed at the difficult Latin of antiquity.

The *Conquest* resembles a Christmas bazaar in having something for everyone, both trash and bargains. If you want sensation you find dreams, visions, prophecies and miracles. The invaders are frightened by phantom armies, a common sight in Ireland. Gerald made use of classical rhetorical speech, which sounds especially implausible in the mouths of Anglo-Norman barons and Irish chieftains. But he also copied documents and records of councils. He provides a superb portrait gallery. His pen-picture of Henry II is unsurpassed and appears in all our textbooks.

It is interesting to compare Gerald with Adam and Helmold as a 'conquest historian'. They have much in common. We find the same ambivalent attitude to the defeated people. Gerald had reason to take the invaders' side. He hoped that an English protectorate over the Irish Church would favour reform and better discipline among the native clergy. His kinsmen, settled in Ireland as colonists, would gain by firmer military support. The Irish struck him as barbarous and inefficient; they had no idea how to manage their affairs. At the same time, like Adam and Helmold, he could sympathize with the conquered and oppressed. He reports atrocities on both sides. The difference between Gerald on the one hand and Adam and Helmold on the other springs from the nature of their stories. The Germans told a success story, slow but final. Gerald recorded a stalemate. Prince John's expedition to Ireland failed; English rule remained partial and imperfect. The Red Indians had resisted the Cowboys to some purpose. A partisan of the invaders had to explain why they lost out to the natives.

To do so he had to analyse causes. First he bows to the altar. We learn from the Old Testament and from later history that God allows no people to be totally destroyed except as a punishment for its sins. Gerald concludes that the Irish were not bad enough nor the invaders good enough to merit total defeat or victory. God had reason to punish both sides. Anyway, the four famous prophets of Irish tradition had

63 An English thirteenth-century illustration to the *Topography of Ireland* by Gerald of Wales. One man kills another with an axe, to indicate the Irish habit of feuding. *Oxford, Bodleian Library, MS Laud. Misc. 720, f.225r*

predicted that the English would never conquer the whole island until Doomsday was approaching. Then Gerald comes down to human causes. Henry II had to leave his conquest incomplete. His sons' rebellion recalled him and he never came back. Turning to John, Gerald again invokes God's displeasure. John had offended God by not helping the Church and he had broken his vow to go on crusade. Gerald goes on to dissect John's political errors. The prince antagonized his Irish allies by not blarneying them: you have to use blarney on the Irish; they expect it. John antagonized the Anglo-Norman and Welsh colonists too. He mocked at their old-fashioned colonial dress and customs and ignored their counsel. He ousted them and installed new men; these wanted only to enrich themselves and were slack in defending their posts. They employed mercenaries, who preferred plunder to fighting.

Then Gerald turns to the techniques of warfare. A wild chaotic country called for trained and experienced troops. Mercenaries were useless there. The Irish had succumbed to the first shock of invasion. Later they learned resistance techniques and had to be fought on their own terrain. Gerald observed that the type of warfare called for in the woods and mountains of Ireland differed from that suitable on the open plains of France, which were more familiar to the Anglo-Normans. Steady cavalry succeeded best on the open plain; light-armed contingents, trained to endure hardship, were needed in Ireland. The type of fighting differed, in that the Irish fought to kill, whereas in France the aim on both sides was to take prisoners in order to win ransom money. It followed in Gerald's view that troops for expeditions to Ireland should be recruited in the Welsh Marches. There, and only there, would you find men accustomed to living and fighting in the conditions they would experience overseas. The voice of Gerald's soldier relatives sounds louder than that of the Divine Judge when it comes to military matters. Hard advice on tactics and recruitment replaces moral considerations.

The *Conquest* ends with a blueprint for the extension of English rule in Ireland and for the government of the subject people. Gerald recommended many sensible measures, such as road-building to give access to rebel areas. He outlined a firm, paternal régime. Tribute from the natives would finance the colonial government. Like so many blueprints it gave a sound recipe for success, but the measures suggested would have cost too much for the government to carry through. A scholar had produced a plan worthy to rest in the files of any colonial office. It was not acted upon.

We have seen that conquest worked as a forcing house for historiography. The crusades supplied even stronger heat. I have chosen three of the many crusading historians available: the anonymous author of the *Deeds of the Franks*, William of Tyre and Geoffrey of Villehardouin. They number among the best-known names and they have the interest of contrast: each one represents a new kind of author or else an original treatment of an old type of history.

The Anonymous was an eyewitness of the First Crusade. He seems to have belonged to a Norman family which had settled in Sicily after the Norman conquest of the island. He joined a Sicilian contingent to the crusade led by Bohemond, the bastard son of another Norman-Sicilian noble. Bohemond was his 'lord'. The *Deeds of the Franks* begins with a short account of the Council of Clermont where Urban II proclaimed the crusade. Then comes a résumé of the various expeditions which set out from Europe to Palestine. After this prelude the Anonymous relates his own experiences as a crusader. His story gets as far as the taking of Jerusalem and the election of a king and patriarch to rule over the new kingdom of the Franks. He mentions the crusaders' victory near Ascalon in 1099; he may have died soon afterwards, since the book stops there.

He had probably begun his book during the crusaders' stay at Antioch after their capture of the city. Bohemond, who aimed to create a principality for himself, stayed at Antioch and refused to join in the march to Jerusalem. The Anonymous then transferred his allegiance to Count Raymond of Toulouse. The book was finished at Jerusalem. It emerges from the story that the author was a knight of minor rank; Bohemond trusted him, but he did not belong to the inner circle of leaders. Indeed, he had the outsider's natural distrust of diplomacy behind closed doors. It is surprising that a layman had the skill to write a history in Latin. The Latin of the *Deeds* is grammatical, though informal. The Anonymous had no literary equipment except for memories of the Bible. Perhaps, as often happened to a younger son, he was made a clerk as a small boy and received a clerical education, so as to make his way in the Church and leave the family estate to his elders. Their deaths might have released him to take up a secular career. Otherwise there is the possibility that a clerk helped him to write. In either case, he speaks to us simply and directly with a freshness of vision which is all his own.

The *Deeds of the Franks* is the first history written in Latin by a layman since Einhard and Nithard wrote in the early ninth century. (Caffaro of Genoa comes a little later.) The Anonymous is unique in his way, like Galbert of Bruges. The *Deeds* became famous as a primary source for the First Crusade; but clerical authors found the presentation too crude and rewrote it in more literary styles. The contrast with conventional histories strikes us at the very beginning. The Anonymous dispenses with a prologue and plunges straight into his story. He did not know or chose to ignore that an author was supposed to apologize for writing at all, for writing inadequately and for giving offence by his truthfulness.

Perhaps the religious purpose of the *Deeds* made the reason for writing it self-evident. The recovery of the Holy Sepulchre was a sequel to Christ's death and resurrection and to the passions of the saints. The crusade swelled the ranks of the martyrs. The Anonymous counted as martyrs all soldier-pilgrims who fell in the holy war. On the siege of Antioch he writes:

More than a thousand of our knights and foot-soldiers were martyred on one day. They ascended into heaven, rejoicing and shining white in their martyrs' robes, glorifying and magnifying our God, One and Three, in whose name they had triumphed. They cried out with one voice: 'Why dost thou not defend our blood, which we shed in thy name?'

He is alluding to a text of Revelation, where the new martyrs are bidden to rest for a while, 'until [the number of] their fellow servants and brethren, who are to be slain even as they, shall be filled up' (6:11). The Turks who were killed by the crusaders 'received everlasting death, giving up their wretched souls to the devil and Satan's ministers'. Local Palestinian martyrs appear in the sky to comfort Christ's soldiers when the Turks press them hard.

The Anonymous sets the pattern for what follows in his account of the Council of Clermont:

When the time had come which our lord Jesus Christ daily shows to the faithful, in the gospel especially, saying *If any man will come after me, let him deny himself and take up his cross and follow me*, a mighty movement spread through all the regions of Gaul.

Christ's enemies and his saints were timeless and unmistakable. The writer's time scale and values are those of the child who said: 'The Bads killed Jesus, and they killed my uncle too in the War.' The very structure of the *Deeds* shows that it was intended to be read aloud as a religious piece. Each book closes with a doxology to mark the end of reading for the day.

The pious purpose goes with vivid reporting. The Anonymous understood military techniques as the average clerical writer could not do. We climb the walls of Antioch by night; the custodian of three towers has betrayed them secretly to Bohemond. The ladder breaks as we climb and we enter by a narrow gate in the wall, feeling for it in the dark. We march over waterless mountains. We smell the stench of corpses piled up in the streets. We hear the Turkish battle cry 'as they suddenly shriek, shout and gabble some devilish word in their own tongue'. The author diverts us, when we get tired of battles, by taking us to the Turkish side to hear what Turkish leaders said about the Franks. His report of their conversation recalls the scene in *Henry V* where Shakespeare makes the French nobles say rude things about the English invaders. The Turkish prince's mother plays the traditional part of the wife who foresees the consequences of her husband's plans and warns him to no avail. The Saracen lady of the *Deeds* has a remarkable knowledge of biblical prophecies and a strange ignorance of the Koran. These asides are wishful thinking; but they make good entertainment.

The Anonymous's own impressions come through when he describes the foreigners with whom he came into contact. The Greeks get short shrift; they were hereditary enemies of the Normans in Sicily. The Palestinian Christians – Syrians and Armenians for the most part – are little people, who emerge from their holes as soon as they can safely sell victuals to the crusaders at the highest price they can get. They were not warriors. The Turks were. They made worthy foes when the two warrior races, the Turks and the Franks, confronted one another. The Anonymous labels his characters to help his hearers, as in vernacular epic. They needed reminding of the character's role when the story was taken up again. All are types, of course. The Greek emperor is 'the wicked'; Bohemond is 'prudent' or 'wise' until he stays behind at Antioch, after which he becomes plain 'Bohemond'. The Turks, more easily recognizable, are called 'wicked' or 'infidel' only occasionally. It must be added that the Anonymous impartially mentions cases of cowardice and indiscipline among the Franks. His prejudices were too securely built into his mind to need propping up by the suppression of facts. Some scholars have detected a change in his attitude towards the end. He began to think more of the material as distinct from the religious rewards of his pilgrimage, telling with glee how the crusaders at last found plentiful food supplies and booty. That is rather an armchair view. An army marches on its stomach. The crusade was a war like any other. The men had gone through such hardships as to deserve their comforts when the time came.

Was the Anonymous a 'typical' second-rank crusader? Can we generalize from his outlook as expressed in the *Deeds*? I doubt it. The mere fact of his writing a history differentiates him from his companions. Maybe he reflects their naïve impressions of what the crusade was about. He was more gifted than they were, probably more thoughtful, and perhaps more religious. At least he tells us how it felt to go on crusade in the first fervour and to share in the first victories.

Turning from him to William of Tyre is like reading John of Salisbury after Galbert or Caffaro. We come back to the study and the court. Some eighty years have passed; subsequent crusades have done little to help the Latin kingdom. The story of the Latins in Palestine provokes sadness rather

than triumph. William of Tyre's *History of Deeds Done Beyond the Sea* is not original in form as was the unique *Deeds of the Franks*. It is a literary, learned history written by an archbishop. It is remarkable for having achieved as much as this kind of history could. William stands out as the mellowest and wisest historian of the Middle Ages.

William's family were colonists settled 'Overseas'. These crusading-state colonists came of landholding families, and belonged to an international network of relatives and their friends. William gives us his intellectual credentials for writing his history in an account of his journey to the West to get himself educated. He spent nearly twenty years as a

65 Bohemond's siege of Antioch on the First Crusade, from a copy of a French version of William of Tyre's *History*, produced in the capital of the dwindling crusader state at Acre, about 1280. *Lyons, Bibliothèque Municipale, MS 828, f.33ͬ*

student in France and Italy (1145/6–65), choosing the best masters of the Liberal Arts, philosophy, theology and civil and canon law. On returning to the Latin kingdom, he received his first preferment, a prebend in the cathedral church of Tyre. The king of Jerusalem, Amalric, took a fancy to him and wished to provide him with more bene-fices; but certain difficulties prevented it. William rose at court. He became chancellor of the kingdom and arch-bishop of Tyre (1174/5). Amalric employed him as his confidential adviser and as tutor to his son. The archbishop went on diplomatic missions to Rome and Byzantium. He fell from court favour after Amalric's death, thereby missing promotion to the patriarchate of Jerusalem, which he had long hoped for. He withdrew to Tyre in disappointment in 1180. Better prospects opened at court when his friends there got the upper hand; but he died about 1185, too soon to get his promotion, and happily for him too soon also to witness Saladin's capture of Jerusalem. He had foreseen it with dread.

The *History* grew slowly out of conversations with Amalric. This king had a passion for listening to accounts of the deeds of rulers and heroic tales. He suggested that William should write up his own deeds as king of Jerusalem. The history of his reign proved to be the middle of a more comprehensive work. It was decided that William should incorporate Amalric's deeds into a general history of Over-seas. So far there were histories of the separate crusades, but no general account of the kingdom. The task involved research on a large scale. William began with the Muslim conquest of Syria from the Byzantines (634–40) and worked onward. His retreat to Tyre gave him leisure for writing. He finished twenty-two books and then broke off, disgusted at the state of affairs: the plight of his country filled him with gloom. His friends, however, persuaded him to continue. He started on book twenty-three, which was interrupted by his death. His other historical work was a *History of the Princes of the East*, written at Amalric's request. It is lost; we shall never know what a thoughtful Latin made of Oriental history. His qualifications for writing were his good classical education, gained in the Western schools, his knowledge of Greek, Arabic and perhaps a little Hebrew, picked up for practical purposes, and his experience as a diplomat and statesman. He took part in the events he describes after his return from the West in 1165, and belonged to the inner power group for most of the time.

66 Opposite: a picture of the precincts of the church of the Holy Sepulchre at Jerusalem, from a guide for pilgrims written in the Cistercian monastery of Reun in the early thirteenth century. Constantine's basilica is at the top. At the bottom is the circular church of the Resurrection, with the supposed tomb of Christ in the centre surrounded by hanging lamps. Between the two, the small structure with a gable shelters the rock of Calvary. Between it and the basilica is a shrine containing the cup of the Last Supper, and to the left another shrine for the table of the Last Supper. *Vienna, Österreichische Nationalbibliothek, MS 609, f.4r*

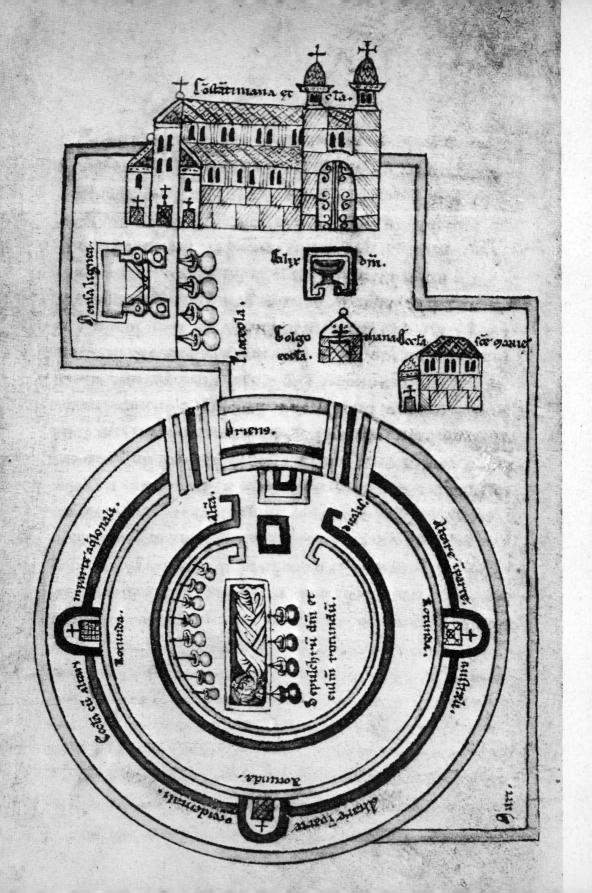

William's cultural background distinguishes him from the Westerners. The Latin colonists had to live with their neighbours. There was friction with Byzantium, but also diplomatic exchanges and marriage alliances. The Greeks proved themselves to be too useful as allies to be dismissed as mere saboteurs of the crusades. Similarly there were truces and traffic with Islam. Many Saracens stayed on after the conquest. In Palestine the Latins came into touch with people at a higher rather than a more primitive level than they had reached. They appreciated Arab learning and skills. Arab doctors could provide better treatment than the Latins, especially for Oriental diseases. The ladies came to rely on 'Jews, Samaritans, Syrians and Arabs' to care for their health; their men followed suit. Their live-and-let-live attitude scandalized newcomers to Overseas. The colonists for their part felt a natural hostility to new pilgrims and settlers: 'You don't understand our problems.' The kingdom of Jerusalem belonged to them. They spent their lives in defending it, a longer time than the few months or years which sufficed for a crusade. Palestine became their home. They got used to the pinkish-grey colours of the Judaean desert and to the dark green valleys which they saw from their fortified towns and castles. Unlike many colonists, they could identify themselves with their country's past. Almost every place-name rang a bell: Mount Sinai, Bethlehem, Nazareth. These were peopled by memories from the Bible and from pagan and Christian antiquity. Interest in the history of Palestine led to more contacts with the natives. Christians would tap local knowledge in order to learn more about the holy places and the legends clustered round them. So the Latin state was more than a kingdom to the colonists settled there; they annexed it as their *patria*, their country. To go West was to go abroad. To return, as William did after his studies, was to come home.

William formulated the idea of *patria*. It gave him the emotional drive which he needed to write his long history. Love of his country has moved many a historian; but in the twelfth century it was new. *Patria* in the Middle Ages often had a religious meaning: we are wayfarers *in via*, travelling to our true *patria* in heaven. When used in a non-religious sense, it meant 'region' or 'place of birth', as on our passport forms. The Romans understood patriotism; men died for their country. Classical studies kept the ancient sense of *patria* alive; but it had no focus. Historians wrote up the deeds of a people or of a ruling house, not the story of their land. It seems odd that patriotism should have focused first on Overseas, with its mixed population, its loose government and its dicey future. Its very exposure may have sharpened the colonists' sense of possession. Love of his country is not a mere classical memory in William's *History*, but a live, anxious feeling. It comes out in his prologues, where otherwise he gives the familiar reasons for composition. He cannot allow the last hundred years to fall out of mind, because love of his country spurs him on. 'The sweetness of our native earth' must outweigh his inadequacy as a historian.

The second prologue at the beginning of his unfinished last book explains his reasons for taking up the tale. There was much to dissuade him. Nobody, he says, would wish to dwell on his country's sickness and failures, whereas it comes naturally to a historian to praise her with all his might. Just now he has nothing praiseworthy to tell. William fell back on Livy's claim to have described the purity and courage of the ancient Romans to their decadent children. Then his friends heartened him by pointing out that both Livy and Josephus had recounted disasters as well as victories when they told their stories of the Romans and the Jews. More-over, the annalist, by virtue of his office, sets down what happened, not what he would like to have happened. So William embarked on his tale of disaster. To write of a country which was loved and threatened called for un-common virtuosity.

His merit as a classicist is that he has mastered his ancient sources. They supply pat quotations, but not too many. He moulded the Suetonian portrait of a ruler to suit his structure: first, a narrative of the foundation of the Latin kingdom in its setting of the Muslim conquest, and then the First Crusade; second, a character sketch of each king, followed by a chronological account of his reign. He knits them together so that the ruler's character is seen to react on current events: a rash king endangered the army. The kings of Jerusalem come to life. It was not William's fault that none of them was as photogenic as Henry II. Other characters are pencilled in, and places too. William gives a geographical account and a history, going back to antiquity, of each place that he mentions. His *History* portrays a land as well as its Frankish conquerors. He worked hard to collect and sift information on what had happened when he was not present as an eye-witness. If his informants' reports varied, he set down each version, as the best he could do. He tried to write objectively, at the risk of annoying contemporaries. Mistakes in tactics or politics and irresponsible behaviour get their share of blame. Nor does he spare his own feelings. It must have cost William dear to tell how King Amalric suddenly asked him to give reasons for the doctrine of the resurrection of the body. Amalric protested that he believed the doctrine; but he wanted to know by what arguments one could prove it to a person who did not accept it on faith alone. It grieved the archbishop's very soul that a Christian prince, son of Christian parents, should question so universally accepted an article of the Creed. He tells us about the conversation nonetheless, to illustrate the king's habit of talking when he had a touch of fever and wanted company to while away the time in bed. William does full justice to the excitement and pathos of his story of Overseas. A flash of eastern magic lights up his description of a caliph's palace as it was described to him. He gives a first-hand and pathetic account of how he discovered that his pupil, the young heir to the kingdom, had contracted leprosy.

William had the defects and prejudices to be looked for in a prelate of the Church. He disliked campaigning in person and disapproved of military bishops. Hence he is at his weakest on military history. He gives bad marks to princes who whittled down ecclesiastical privileges. The archbishop naturally resented the liberties of the religious orders, and of the Knights Templar in particular, because their exemption from diocesan control created difficulties. His jealousy of the Templars prevents him from giving them due credit for their share in defending the kingdom. He is surprisingly objective in his judgments otherwise.

The problem of causation brought out William's best qualities as a historian. Pope Urban II's call to crusade brightened the darkness of troubled times and raised new hopes for Christendom. But William probed the Anonymous' account of the 'mighty movement' which launched the First Crusade. Not every crusader acted out of religious fervour. Some took the cross because their friends did, so as not to seem cowardly, some just for the fun of it, and some to avoid being dunned by their creditors; others were criminals, escaping from justice. The First Crusade succeeded in spite of these mixed motives. On reaching the year 1174, William looked back to ask himself why success had not continued: why did the present generation fail to maintain the conquests of their forbears Overseas? The obvious answer was 'moral decline'. This may have been wrong: the Franks in Palestine had grown more comfort-loving, and moralists normally equate comfort with sinfulness; it did not follow that the colonists had degenerated. But his *passe-partout* explanation did not satisfy William either. He sought other reasons in Muslim history. The first crusaders were expert soldiers, attacking a country whose natives had grown accustomed to peace and had forgotten how to defend themselves. Their enemies were disunited politically. The Muslim princes fought one another instead of obeying a superior. Almost every city had its own lord. Hence these isolated strongholds fell easily to the crusaders. Now, on the contrary, the Muslims were united under one ruler. The sultan had plenty of money, thanks to his conquests, and could pay his troops. Recruits were at hand in quantity, given the means to hire them. The present generation of Franks Overseas faced much greater odds than their forbears.

William realized that political unity and a full treasury will decide a conflict between two states. Modern historians of the Latin kingdom still subscribe to William's analysis of the causes of its fall. They refine upon his account by pointing to the special weaknesses of Latin government Overseas: the king lacked financial resources and his control over his barons grew looser during the twelfth century. General acceptance of William's theory of causes is the compliment paid to him as a historian.

Geoffrey of Villehardouin resembled the Anonymous in being a layman and a soldier. His *Conquest of Constantinople*, like the Anonymous's *Deeds of the Franks*, is an eyewitness account and a success story. Both writers planned their story in much the same way: both begin with the preaching of the crusade; they go on to describe the expedition and its victorious outcome; they round off by reporting its aftermath. There the likenesses end. Villehardouin, marshal of Champagne, was no simple knight, but a leader and organizer. He got his share in the spoils of the Fourth Crusade. After the capture of Constantinople he held the office of marshal in the new Latin empire and received the principate of Acaia in Greece for himself and his heirs.

Geoffrey wrote his book in French. The *Conquest of Constantinople* is the earliest French historical prose narrative surviving today. The absence of precedents for comparison means that the *Conquest* bristles with problems for the

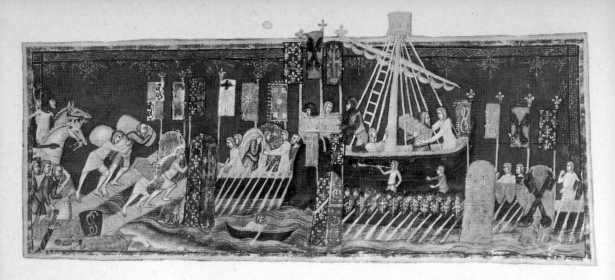

modern historian. We do not know what the author had
read. He had grasped the outlines of earlier crusading
histories and he must have listened to vernacular epics and
romances. He borrows their literary conventions, telling his
audience to 'listen carefully' and repeating 'as the book says'
to authenticate his story. But he was no romancer. He told
the true and marvellous tale of the conquest of a hitherto
impregnable city, packed full of treasure, by a small army.
Rhetoric and miracle stories would have spoilt his effect. He
had a sharp eye for military detail and he excels in conveying
a fresh direct impression of what he saw. Speechifying bored
him. Although he took part in the leaders' councils, he
contented himself with a brief summary of what was said
there and does not embroider by rhetoric.

His purpose in writing is equally open to question.
Historians of French medieval literature have classified the
Conquest as a 'failed epic'. On this view, Geoffrey planned to
write an epic on the crusaders' victory; but he ended with a
wretched anticlimax. The conquerors failed to deal with
Greek resistance in the countryside and in the smaller towns
of their empire. This view of the *Conquest* is unconvincing.
If Geoffrey had wanted to write a prose epic, he could have
stopped while the going was good. The capture of Constantinople would have made a fine ending. Moreover, an
epic should have heroes, and he does not supply them. It is
true that the doge of Venice plays an honourable role in the
Conquest; but the blind old man, though wise and coura-
geous in Geoffrey's eyes, cannot star as a hero. We might
ascribe the star part to Geoffrey himself, but he does not
write to magnify his own exploits at the expense of others.

He mentions his name and his contribution to warfare and diplomacy without depriving his friends of glory.

A historian's view of the *Conquest* is that it was written as propaganda. Geoffrey wanted to cover up the plot which led to the diversion of the crusade to besiege and capture a Christian capital. This view is more plausible. Not all of Geoffrey's contemporaries regarded the Fourth Crusade as a glorious victory. Some saw it as a dirty business from the start. The pope had forbidden attacks on Christians; but the Venetians had the whip-hand and defied his ban. They had undertaken to provide shipping for the expedition, which set off from Venice. The crusaders could not pay the sum agreed upon; hence they had to comply with the Venetians' plans if they used the Venetian fleet. Constantinople was the main obstacle to the Venetian policy of commercial expansion. The doge and his compatriots made use of the crusaders' greed for land and booty in order to exploit a dynastic quarrel within the city. The crusade was diverted, Constantinople was taken, and a Latin empire set up there. In fact the Venetians had incurred excommunication before ever they set foot on Byzantine soil, since they had obliged the crusaders to help them to capture the Christian city of Zara in Dalmatia on their way down the Adriatic. The pope did not insist on the ban for fear of losing what little control over the crusade that he had.

Geoffrey certainly distorts his story by suppressing some known facts. He camouflages the Venetians' stake in the conquest of Constantinople and their excommunication. He gives an unfair account of the split in the crusaders' leadership. The truth was that none of the leaders had any intention of taking their troops to the Holy Land. To do so would have been romatic nonsense and would not have helped the kingdom of Acre. The intention was to strike at Saracen power at its strongest point, the naval bases in Egypt. The rank-and-file of crusaders, on the other hand, looked forward to going on an armed pilgrimage to the Holy Land of the old-fashioned type. The leaders deliberately misled their men by giving out that the expedition was going 'overseas'; its precise destination was not specified. Geoffrey tells us so honestly. The split came when it was proposed to divert the expedition to Constantinople. Some of the leaders dug their toes in. They refused to accompany the Venetians and the other crusaders. As they were too few in number to attack Egypt, the objectors set out for Palestine to do what they

68 Crusaders proceed to Constantinople by sea, from a late thirteenth-century French copy of Villehardouin. *Paris, Bibliothèque Nationale, MS fr. 12203, f.78v*

69 The Dominican Burchard of Monte Sion wrote a *Description of the Holy Land* in 1283 which excelled in detail and scientific precision. In this miniature from a Venetian manuscript of Burchard's work we see Christian warriors at Jerusalem. *Padua, Biblioteca del Seminario, MS 74, f.13v*

could. Geoffrey represents them as saboteurs of the crusade. He describes them as 'those who wanted to disband the army'. The 'true crusaders' were Geoffrey and his friends. He ignores the religious motives of those who scrupled to make war on their fellow-Christians. It must be admitted that he was correct in saying that they achieved little in Palestine.

It would be wrong, however, to dismiss the *Conquest* as mere propaganda. Research on the tangled story of intrigue leading up to the diversion suggests that there was no 'plot' to be covered up. The Venetians could not have plotted the diversion because they were not in a position to foresee what would happen. There were too many dangers. Hard bargaining and cunning opportunism explain their conduct better than deep scheming in advance. In any case, the Latin empire was a *fait accompli* when Geoffrey wrote the *Conquest* in 1207. The pope had recognized it. Geoffrey had no reason to apologize for the Venetians and their allies among the crusaders, though he tried to conceal the discreditable side of the diversion to Constantinople.

The most recent and probable view of the *Conquest* is simpler: the book belongs to the 'War Memoirs of a Successful General' class. Geoffrey gives us bias rather than falsification, which is what one would expect in a book of the kind. This view also disposes of the 'failed epic' theory. It comes naturally to a general to record mopping-up operations after a victory, as Geoffrey does. They are not an anticlimax to a soldier's mind; and a general can easily underrate the strength of resistance movements, as Geoffrey underrated Greek resistance to the Latins.

His memoirs are precious as a new genre, and all the more so for having been written by a layman. They show us a mind and outlook much more secular than the Anonymous's. Geoffrey takes so little interest in religion and morals that he does not even bother to criticize the clergy. Papal meddling in military matters just irritated him; clerical quarrels amused him. The two papal legates who went with the crusaders were both Cistercian abbots. One sided with 'the true crusaders', as Geoffrey calls them, the other opposed the diversion. The difference between the two abbots and legates struck Geoffrey as comic.

He has his own theory of causation: it is a simple fatalism. Whatever happens is God's will. This opinion blocked the way to any subtle analysis of causes. His secular outlook did not make for deep thinking.

We turn now to the Albigensian Crusade, directed against the heretics in southern France. These heretics left no histories or chronicles, which is not surprising. The Cathars were dualists: they believed that the devil had created the visible world. To write its history, therefore, would have been mere muckraking. Another group of heretics, known as the Waldenses (from their leader, Valdès) or 'Poor Men of Lyons', were more like Protestants in their beliefs. Perhaps they did produce a historian of their sect; if so, his work has not survived. Probably they were kept too busy disputing with Cathars and Catholics to turn their minds to history. We depend on Catholic historiographers to tell the story of the crusades against there heretics in the Midi. Fortunately for us, they approach it from very different points of view.

Our first author is a Cistercian monk, Peter of the abbey of Vaux de Cernai. His uncle, the abbot, took Peter with him when he went on the Fourth Crusade as papal legate. This was the legate branded by Geoffrey of Villehardouin as a saboteur, because he persisted in going on to the Holy Land. In 1212, when the uncle and nephew had returned, Innocent III appointed the abbot of Cernai as his legate on the Albigensian Crusade (the popes frequently used Cistercian monks to serve as legates and missionaries to the heretics). The abbot took Peter with him again. So Peter had two kinds of crusading experience. He took part in campaigns, though as a monk he did not actually fight.

The crusade against the Albigensians had a lightning success. The barons of northern France cut through the unprepared, undisciplined forces of the Midi, as a knife cuts into cheese. The southern nobles were dispossessed of their lands. The crusading leader Simon de Montfort (father of the Earl Simon who fell at the battle of Evesham) carved out a principality for himself. Peter's uncle became bishop of Carcassonne in 1214. His nephew may have stayed with him to serve him as secretary. At any rate, Peter spent most

70 Tomb-slab of Simon de Montfort, killed while he was laying siege to Toulouse in June, 1218. He was buried in the church of St Nazaire at Carcassonne.

of his time in the Midi after 1212. There he wrote his Latin *History of the Albigensian Crusades*. It breaks off at 1218. Perhaps Peter died, or perhaps he stopped writing because Simon de Montfort was killed in that year. Simon was Peter's hero. His admiration for Simon went back to the Fourth Crusade, when Simon led the contingent which made for Palestine.

The *History of the Albigensian Crusades* is a full, detailed narrative, set out in chronological order. Peter had a gift for observation and description. He has been called 'a great painter of ruins'; there were plenty to paint in the devastated area of the *terra Albigensium*. He had a soldier's delight in good fortifications. The town of Carcassonne pleased him as a citadel, even when it was still in enemy hands. We can see vividly from his comments how the unaccustomed scenery and ways of the Midi struck a northerner. If we compare him with historians of the crusades to Palestine, Peter comes closest to the anonymous author of the *Deeds of the Franks*. He regards the heretics in the same way as the Anonymous regarded the Muslims. Heretics were devilish. They deserved what they got.

71 Simon de Montfort's siege of Toulouse is represented in a thirteenth-century carving in the same church as Simon's tomb-slab (ill. 70). On the left the crusaders approach in a three-storeyed siege tower. On the right is the beleaguered city, behind a palisade. Some of its citizens, bottom right, are working a great catapult like the one that killed Simon. At the top right one of the besiegers, who has been hauled up by ropes, is hacked to pieces by the defenders; an angel receives his soul.

Peter's avowed purpose in writing is stated in a preface to part one of the *History*, addressed to Pope Innocent III. The *History* would preserve the memory of God's wonderful works: the crusaders had saved the shipwrecked Church in the Midi. Peter's unstated purpose, perhaps suggested by his superiors, was to jog the pope's elbow on behalf of Simon and his allies. Innocent had not envisaged total expropriation of the southern lords by the crusaders. The count of Toulouse appealed to Rome. It looked as though Innocent might favour him. Peter hoped to influence the pope to decide for Simon against the count of Toulouse. It was part of his propaganda to denounce the heretics and to smear the count and other southern nobles as heretics by association. Peter told the truth in stating that they had tolerated heresy on their estates; but they had more complex reasons for doing so than his *History* lets out. Some flirted with heresy; their womenfolk often did more than flirt; but his blanket accusation was unjust.

Peter used the previous history of the Midi to support his case. He traced heresy back to the Visigothic invasion and settlement in the south of France. Toulouse (the capital of the Visigoths) had been a centre of heresy ever since. It did not trouble him that the Visigoths had been Arians, not Mani-chees, or that Arianism was not a dualist creed. His statement that the counts of Toulouse had always been heretics looks odd in the light of their record as crusaders to the Holy Land. Count Raymond played a key part in the First Crusade; his heirs neglected their county in order to follow his example. In making his propaganda, however, Peter had the advantage that he genuinely believed it. He had no understanding of the southern mentality and no sense of humour. It seemed to him incredible that a Catholic could neglect his duty to suppress heresy on his domains. Therefore the counts of Toulouse were heretics. Peter over-simplified.

The same rigid orthodoxy comes out in a short Latin chronicle written by a Dominican inquisitor called William of Pelhisson (d. 1268). He was a southerner by origin; but his office as inquisitor inclined him to give no quarter to heretics. On the other hand, he shows us a different picture from Peter's. The soldier-monk came south with a con-quering army, whereas the Dominican friar had to work among the heretics and the disaffected at risk of his life. He records in simple terms his shared experiences as a member of a small community of friars. A few devout Catholics helped

z ɫ ɫacte se uela solere dicebant. Hec uestibʒ
alliſ utebantur niſi corijſ animaliū inīdū
n magna necessitate. Et cū a nauīs experte

pulsi fuissent. tandem sb insula qdā
medica se receperūt. ū ɫ andatū
morsu finiumqz tphauū inmo mɫ

them by smuggling in food supplies when a hostile populace threatened the brothers with starvation. The pope founded a university at Toulouse in 1229 in order to combat heretical teaching. Catholic doctrine sounded so strange to the students that mocking laughter rang out in the lecture room. A tourist who visits the 'fortress churches' of Languedoc should read William's chronicle. It will show him why the Catholics had to build themselves strongholds to serve as refuges and

72 The fortress church at Albi, begun in 1282, intended to enable the Catholics to defend themselves against heretics and rebels. This view shows the wall-walk and arrow-slits.

Colour plate VIII
See caption p. 148.

73–75 The great Bible picture book, known as the *Bible moralisée*, presents the text of the Scriptures set beside medallions showing both Bible history, what happened, and its allegorical and moral interpretation. These roundels come from two copies of the picture book made in France, probably in the 1230s. The 'moralities' often refer to current events. The spread of heresy led to heart-searching by the clergy.
Right: a lazy priest sleeps while the heretics preach.
Centre: a heretic puts out his tongue at a priest, who is preaching to the people, to illustrate the effrontery of the heretics; they are allowed to go about unmolested.
Far right: the Inquisition is established to destroy heresy. Dominican friars were put in charge of the Inquisition at Toulouse. Here we see a friar interrogating a suspect and then handing him over to the secular arm to be imprisoned or burnt. *Paris, Bibliothèque Nationale, MS lat. 11560, f.11or and 137r; and London, British Museum, MS Harl. 1526, f.30v (far right)*

to stand up to siege. This Dominican took even less interest in the causes of heresy than did Peter of Cernai: the devil was cause enough for him.

The cold light of reason breaks through in our next Latin chronicle. The author, William of Puylaurens, wrote at a date when events could be reviewed more calmly. He was a southerner, like Pelhisson, but not an inquisitor. Puylaurens had the title of Master; we do not know where he studied. He was a secular priest, employed as notary by the bishop of Toulouse. Earlier he had probably worked on the staff of Bishop Fulk of Toulouse, who died in 1231. Then he acted as chaplain to the count of Toulouse. The first part of his book, written after 1249, covers about fifty years of Midi history from the rise of heresy down to the death of his patron, the count of Toulouse. The second part, going down to 1273/4, is a scrappy record, which need not concern us. Puylaurens called his book a chronicle. It is a factual narrative without any pretensions to style. He wrote it for a wide public, not for an élite of scholars or lay nobles. His aim in his own words was

to set down some of those things which I saw or heard from my neighbours, so that men of upper, middle and lower ranks shall understand God's judgments, by which he afflicted these lands in consequence of the sins of their people.

We expect preacher's thunder. Not at all. Puylaurens analysed the causes of heresy. His familiarity with southern

ways gave him a start over Peter of Cernai. The hero of his chronicle is not the dashing Simon de Montfort, but Bishop Fulk of Toulouse, a Cistercian and a pillar of orthodoxy, but wise and witty. Puylaurens loves to quote his repartee. One day, when standing on the walls of Toulouse, he heard some heretics shout up at him that he was 'the devil's bishop'. 'Quite right,' he answered, 'you *are* devils, and I *am* your bishop.' Puylaurens could appreciate the motive behind a political crime. Count Raymond of Toulouse hanged his brother, Count Baldwin. The chronicler excused Baldwin's treachery to his brother – he joined the northerners because Raymond had never done anything for him – but on the other hand Raymond had a political excuse for his fratricide. As a student of politics, Puylaurens pounces on a diplomatic blunder; he can distinguish between propaganda and fact. His sympathies went to the French monarchy in the long run. The Capetians were foreigners to the Midi, but their conquest brought law and order to a troubled country. Puylaurens was a realist.

He diagnosed heresy as a symptom of a moral illness which infected the whole of Midi society. The cause of the illness was negligence: the clergy neglected their duty to teach Catholic doctrine to the people and to set a good example. The heretics had an appearance of goodness. Hence they were able to gain many followers. Dissatisfaction with the Church expressed itself in heresy. This diagnosis has had a long life. 'The corruption of the Church' is still the commonest answer to the question: 'why did heresy make more progress in the Midi than elsewhere?' Only recently have historians begun to doubt whether the Church in the Midi was especially open to criticism and to search for other causes. Puylaurens' answer has done duty for centuries. It may be too simple; but it represents the situation as it seemed to a rational observer.

Puylaurens goes on to discuss the spread of heresy. It was a creeping disease. The sectaries worked in hiding at first; then their success emboldened them to preach openly. He explains what had puzzled newcomers to the Midi, beginning with Peter of Cernai: why did Catholics live side by side with heretics without trying to convert them or persecute them? Peter dismissed them all as heretics to a man. Puylaurens answers that the heretics' success created a vicious circle. The clergy, non-starters in the race for esteem, sank so low that no knight would make his son a clerk. Hence there was a shortage of ordinands. The bishops could not reject unworthy candidates; they 'made clerks as they could'. Clerical standards of learning and conduct deteriorated still more. A Church so poorly staffed could not discipline the laity. The knights of the Midi adhered to whichever sect caught their fancy. The heretics held their conventicles publicly and buried their followers in their own graveyards. Puylaurens' masterly account of the way heresy spread makes it easy to understand why the southern nobles feared to use force. To attack heresy would have meant disturbing the whole *status quo* and would have upset all their subjects, Catholics or sectaries. Puylaurens can convey a situation and he is adept at explanations.

Our last two historiographers are poets writing in Provençal. One began and the other continued the *Song of the Albigensian Crusade*. The first poet tells us that he was a Master of Arts and clerk called William of Tudela (in Spanish Navarre). He earned his living as a professional entertainer and reciter of verses in noble households. He began his poem about 1210 and stopped in 1213, perhaps because his patron, Count Baldwin, was killed by his brother, the count of Toulouse, in that year. There were other historical poems in the vernacular; William of Tudela says that he modelled his on a crusading story, the *Song of Antioch* (now lost). Unfortunately for the reciters, their market was limited and they had to compete with jesters and mimes,

providers of mere slapstick. One had to advertise oneself. This is William's publisher's blurb:

As soon as William started his song he hardly slept till he'd finished. It's well written and full of fine verses. Take the trouble to listen and all of you, great and small, will learn many things, well put and sensible, since the author has his belly full of good sayings. He who doesn't know the poem and hasn't felt its force has no idea what he's missing.

William calls himself 'a clever fellow' and claims to have foretold the disasters hanging over the Midi by means of geomancy, a sort of white magic:

He knew by his study of this science that the land would be burned and ravaged because of the mad beliefs which had been allowed into it, that the rich burghers would be despoiled of their goods and that the knights would depart as exiles to foreign places.

But the tale is told as 'a good yarn'; the tragic side of it only makes it more compelling. The narrator does not compromise himself. The crusaders acted savagely; but it was crazy

76 The twelfth-century tympanum of St Faith at Conques, a centre of pilgrimage for Christendom situated in the Languedoc, shows the Last Judgment and the fate of the damned. In this detail we see on the right a heretic, holding a parchment and book containing heretical doctrine. He is placed with his head below the level of the earth, and a devil shuts his mouth to prevent him from speaking.

155

of the southerners to let heresy spread. The real villains, in his view and doubtless in that of his audience, were the countrymen, who finished off the dying after a battle with sticks and stones in order to rob the corpses. They had no right to interfere in gentlemen's wars. William's theory of causation recalls the *Conquest of Constantinople*: what must be will be; 'what God ordains, that man cannot change.' This is history at the level of a pastime.

A better poet continued the *Song* from 1213 to 1218/19, stopping at the point when the men of Toulouse were preparing to defend their city against Prince Louis of France. He gives us a sample of 'nostalgic history', to use Croce's classification. All we know of the writer has to be deduced from his verses and qualified as 'probable'. He was a Master of Arts and a clerk, like William of Tudela; he was attached to the court of Count Raymond VII of Toulouse, whom he accompanied to the Lateran Council of 1215, when Raymond went to plead for reinstatement to his confiscated lands and rights. The poet wrote soon after 1228. Had he finished the *Song*, he might have given his name at the end. His feelings are in no doubt. He defended the southerners against the crusaders. The anonymous poet was neither a heretic nor anti-papal; he wrote as a good Catholic, believing that God took the side of those who defended their land against foreign enemies. The northerners used the crusade against heresy as an excuse for their greedy attack on the Midi; they pretended that all the southerners were heretics, which was quite untrue. Bishop Fulk of Toulouse, the hero of William of Puylaurens, appears as a mealy-mouthed hypocrite because he collaborated with the crusaders. Simon de Montfort, the hero of Peter of Cernai, had been buried with honour and praised for his holiness. The anonymous poet comments that Simon had 'earned his fame by butchering more women and children than men'.

More was at stake for the southerners than defeat, expropriation and slaughter. The northerners overturned values; a whole way of life came to an end. The poet calls his values *prix et parage*, and personifies them. *Prix* meant prowess or knightly virtue. *Parage* stood for the ranks of the southern courts, which offered due reward for prowess. The knights of the Midi tended to assemble at their lord's court instead of living mainly on their estates, since these were too fragmented to support a family. The ladies of the court attracted 'courtly love' poems. Northern courts favoured a different type of culture, less exotic and brilliant. Ruthless 'levellers' from the North destroyed *prix et parage*. Simon's death brought a moment of hope; *prix et parage* shone out again, but not for long. The next wave of invaders trod them down.

Defeat has its victories in historiography. The historians of conquest and crusade show clearly that defeat is a better teacher than success. Writers who had to tell of defeat or stalemate or the Church's failure to stop the spread of heresy were led by their theme to reflect on causation. Fanaticism gave way to cool appraisal. Moral decay and divine punishment of sin no longer sufficed as the only reasons for failure. Many of our historiographers probe more deeply. Adam of Bremen, Helmold, Gerald of Wales, William of Tyre and William of Puylaurens all look for human agencies when they record setbacks or disasters.

Emotion as well as reason belongs to the very stuff of history. It took utter defeat to bring out the full bitterness which we taste in the second part of the *Song of the Albigensian Crusade*. The conquered speak to us in some histories: Benedict of Monte Soracte described the Saxon conquest of Rome; the *Anglo-Saxon Chronicle* tells of the Danish invasions and of the Norman conquest of England. Neither can compete with the poet of the *Song* as artists in pathos.

es hor
maio p
que no
nos for
aquite
retrain
frucois
mctle
z au l
roi loc

le gros qui tante paine sofri en s
tens q tante bataile forur et rue ses

The thirteenth century: an epilogue

Although the thirteenth century was not a period of experiment in historiography, the traditional genres were developed and some of them took on a new lease of life. The monastic chronicle is an outstanding example. It had its heyday in England in the thirteenth century, to the extent that it colours an Englishman's view of medieval historiography in general. An English student of medieval history is brought up on Jocelyn of Brakelonde and Matthew Paris. One represents local and the other 'world' history.

Jocelyn's *Deeds of Abbot Samson* of Bury St Edmunds in Suffolk is too well known to need description here. No writer of any time can beat Jocelyn as a portrayer of character: we come to know Abbot Samson better than any thirteenth-century English abbot, thanks to his biographer. We experience the reactions of the monks of Bury to his masterful rule. We live with them and share in their hopes and fears for the well-being of their community. The *Deeds of Abbot Samson* offers full scope to students who want to understand the workings of both local and central government in the early thirteenth century, since Jocelyn gives precious details on the relations between the king and the abbey on the one hand and between the abbey and its tenants on the other.

An anonymous writer from Bury did almost as well as Jocelyn in *The Election of Hugh*, an account of a disputed election to the abbacy of Bury towards the end of King John's reign (1199–1216). Both authors introduce us to the same quarrelsome, self-regarding community. Both describe the nervousness of the monks when the cold draught of royal anger blows through. The author of *The Election of Hugh* does not set out to portray character in the round as Jocelyn had done; he sketches in his *personae* more lightly, but persuasively. Both authors catch the excitement of the formation of parties among the brethren. The disputed election described in the second book gave the younger, more daring monks a chance to uphold the liberties of the

77 Opposite: a scene from the *Great Chronicles of France* (see p. 162). King Louis VII remonstrates with the burghers of Orleans, who want to found a commune. His counsellors back him up. From a thirteenth-century translation of the *Chronicles* by the monk Primat of St Denis (see ill. 79). *Paris, Bibliothèque Ste Geneviève, MS 782, f.26v*

abbey by demanding a free election. The older, more timid brothers and the waverers opposed them for fear of the king. The prior, a character familiar to all members of a tightly knit group at any time, was on whichever side had spoken to him last. The reader draws a sigh of relief when the abbey passes unscathed through its ordeal.

Other abbeys had their historians. To mention one only: Master Thomas of Marlborough in Wiltshire wrote a chronicle of Evesham, also in the early thirteenth century. The core of his work consists of an account of a lawsuit. Here, too, there were activists and defeatists among the monks. In spite of the length and tedium of the litigation, Thomas succeeds in holding our interest: will the abbey win its case? Eventually the appeal to Rome went in favour of Evesham. Thomas, who attended in person to plead for his abbey, was so overcome by exhaustion and joy that he fell fainting at the pope's feet.

True craftsmanship has gone into these local histories. A reader who wants to appreciate it should try his hand at writing up his own experiences of life in an institution. It is more difficult than it seems at first sight to make them sound colourful and important.

Matthew Paris (d. 1259) produced both local and 'world' history. His mammoth output surpassed anything ever attempted in a Benedictine abbey. I shall concentrate on his *Greater Chronicle*, since that is the most famous of his historical works. Its scope and volume are amazing. Scholars use it as a primary source for both English and European history. The author had his roots in the abbey of St Alban. Matthew

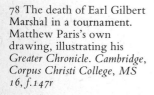

78 The death of Earl Gilbert Marshal in a tournament. Matthew Paris's own drawing, illustrating his *Greater Chronicle. Cambridge, Corpus Christi College, MS 16, f.147r*

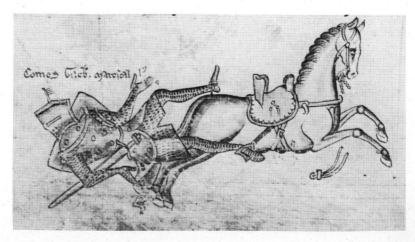

describes his fellow Benedictines as 'good brothers, whose hearts were set on prayer and hospitality'. Their duties as hosts put them in the way of collecting news. St Alban's is situated on the main road north from London; it was an ideal repository for information of all kinds. Matthew made the most of his opportunities. He had an unquenchable thirst for news and gossip, which combined with the passion of an archivist. He copied documents concerning the items he recorded, and copied so extensively that he had to find a special place for documents in his 'book of additions' to the *Chronicle*. His other gifts were a flair for writing and artistic skill. For Matthew was also an artist: he illustrated his text with bold, expressive drawings. That was a rare and personal juxtaposition. Very few authors made their own illustrations in the Middle Ages.

Matthew Paris's outstanding achievement was to put across his point of view. The vast quantity of facts which he assembled would have made his chronicle a valley of dry bones, if they had not passed through his lively mind. We see them as he did. Matthew had the nerve to let himself go. He selected, distorted, invented and commented. His chronicle presents a set of opinions and prejudices shared by other English chroniclers. Roger of Wendover, his predecessor at St Alban's, had already expressed them in a less coherent way. The great English abbeys represented an early, uncoordinated version of the 'country party' versus the 'court party' or the 'outs' versus the 'ins'. Office at court, including government office, spelled power, influence and riches. The Black Monks had no footing at court. Few became bishops in the thirteenth century. This weakened their pull at the other power centre of Christendom, the papal court. The abbeys felt the pressure of royal and papal taxation. The popes also aimed to tighten up discipline and observance in the exempt abbeys by appointing visitors, often the diocesan bishop, to enquire into the running of the house and to correct abuses.

The monks resented what they saw as exploitation and interference. They found themselves at the receiving end of the bureaucracy. Nobody likes tax-collectors, nosy parkers and money-lenders. Their being 'foreigners' added fuel to the flame; Henry III employed foreign favourites in his government. Hence monastic chroniclers tend to xenophobia and favour native opposition movements. The new orders of mendicant friars put the monks' noses out of joint too. The rise of universities left them in an intellectual back-water. Matthew's writings reflect a reaction against new movements in general. His bias is so obvious as to be self-defeating and his prejudices cancel each other out. The friars made him jealous; the reforming zeal of Robert Grosseteste, bishop of Lincoln, annoyed him. On the other hand, as an Englishman he took pride in Oxford University. Scholar-bishops and friars appealed to him so long as they kept away from St Alban's. Matthew could be careless and inaccurate as a chronicler; that is a defect. His bias stamps his personality on his story. Slapdash judgments are part of it. We must take a genius as we find him.

Matthew's *Greater Chronicle* has no rival on the continent of Europe. The monks of St Denis, however, achieved some-thing else. They became official historiographers of the French monarchy. Suger's attempts to identify his abbey with the royal house bore fruit: a royal chronicle began to be kept in the early thirteenth century, or perhaps even earlier, and was added to. A monk of St Denis called Primat trans-lated the compilation into French in 1274. The French copies, lavishly illustrated, came to be known as the *Great Chronicles of France*. England had nothing comparable. Westminster Abbey had much the same status as St Denis in the thirteenth century. Its chroniclers took the royal side in contrast to the other abbeys, which were normally opposition-minded; yet Westminster never produced an authorized royal version of English history.

The mendicant friars contributed their share to histori-ography: friaries kept annals and chronicles. The Franciscans especially breathed new life into the genre of saints' lives. Memories of their founder and disputes on the interpretation of their Rule supplied the driving force. The inspiration spilled over into *The Coming of the Friars Minor to England* by Thomas of Eccleston. Thomas studied at Paris as a secular clerk, joined the order in England about 1230, continued his studies at the Oxford Greyfriars and was later transferred to London. He finished his chronicle, which contained material collected over some twenty-five years, about 1258/9.

Thomas's chronicle is a religious piece. He divided it into homilies, to be read aloud to the friars. He wanted to rekindle the joyous simplicity and delight in poverty of the first Franciscans, true sons of St Francis. Since 'examples touch the heart more than words', he gives many examples, inserting them into his biographies of the men who played

79 The monk Primat presents his translation of the *Great Chronicles of France* to King Philip III. The abbot of St Denis and monks of the abbey stand behind Primat. *Paris, Bibliothèque Ste Geneviève, MS 782, f.326v*

an important part in the order in England in its early days. His chronicle gives an idealized, nostalgic picture of the first comers and of their hardships in the Oxford schools and elsewhere. An inner tension enlivens his tale. He praises their poverty, but loves to record gifts made to the friars, the addition of books to their libraries, the building of convents and their removal to larger, healthier sites. The history of any religious order had to include the history of its endowment.

Matthew Paris's opposite number in Italy was a Franciscan, Fra Salimbene, who compiled a bulky chronicle covering the period from about 1168 to 1304. His curiosity equalled Matthew's; his circumstances as a member of a mobile, international order gave him different means of quenching his thirst for new items. He could go round collecting them himself, when his superiors sent him on business or transferred him to other friaries, instead of waiting for news to come to him. Salimbene gossiped with all sorts of people, from popes down to beggars. He and Matthew have different gifts as writers. Matthew can convey a scene; Salimbene can describe an object so well that one can almost see it and touch it. He has no 'message', either religious or political, unless it be the message that a good Franciscan can enjoy just being alive. Observation concerned him more than religious observance. He was against the emperor Frederick II as a persecutor of the Church, but he had no illusions about churchmen.

163

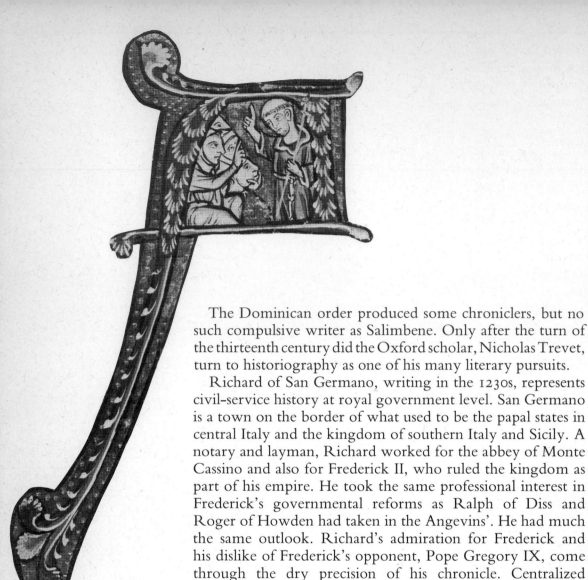

The Dominican order produced some chroniclers, but no such compulsive writer as Salimbene. Only after the turn of the thirteenth century did the Oxford scholar, Nicholas Trevet, turn to historiography as one of his many literary pursuits.

Richard of San Germano, writing in the 1230s, represents civil-service history at royal government level. San Germano is a town on the border of what used to be the papal states in central Italy and the kingdom of southern Italy and Sicily. A notary and layman, Richard worked for the abbey of Monte Cassino and also for Frederick II, who ruled the kingdom as part of his empire. He took the same professional interest in Frederick's governmental reforms as Ralph of Diss and Roger of Howden had taken in the Angevins'. He had much the same outlook. Richard's admiration for Frederick and his dislike of Frederick's opponent, Pope Gregory IX, come through the dry precision of his chronicle. Centralized bureaucracy in the interest of law and order pleased him; but he turned sour on the emperor when he sacrificed his Sicilian subjects to his imperial policy and bled them to pay for his campaigns outside the kingdom. Just as Ralph of Diss preferred Henry II to his more flashy son, so Richard of San Germano preferred Frederick the Wise as king of Sicily to the same Frederick as emperor with imperial ambitions.

No royal clerk in England took up the story of government where Roger of Howden left off. Angevin bureaucracy had passed through its heroic age. We hear of it mainly from its critics. Chroniclers approved of Edward I's reforms, but his advisers let others use them as historical material. The fact of government impinged on historiography at all levels.

Town chroniclers record the changes in local affairs and their dealings with other towns. Papal biographers deal with papal administration and finance. The merchant banker enters into history as one of its makers.

The Paris schools of the late twelfth century inspired a type of historiography which can be termed 'pulpit history'. Master Peter, chanter of Notre Dame, known as 'Peter the Chanter' (d. 1197), gathered around him a group of pupils and colleagues dedicated to preaching. They included Master Stephen Langton, who taught at Paris *c.* 1180–1206 and died as archbishop of Canterbury in 1228. The Chanter and his friends preached in person to clergy and people. They also taught in the schools that a master of the Holy Page had a duty to preach when he left Paris to take up the cure of souls elsewhere. Practical training went with the call to evangelize. It was given through the medium of lectures on the Bible. Lectures deriving from the Chanter and his circle often read like sermons or homilies. The master satirizes society: he holds up a mirror where various ranks of the hierarchy, prelates, princes and their subjects, whether clerk or lay, can see how they ought to behave and how far they fall short of the ideal. The message would carry better if the lecturer or preacher made it amusing; so he mixed grave and gay by telling stories and making jokes or pawky allusions.

This preacher's mentality conditioned the approach to history. A scholar trained in the Chanter's milieu would stress the exemplarist value of history not only in his preface, as was customary, but in his selection and presentation of events throughout his story.

James of Vitry was a devoted pupil of Peter the Chanter, whom he describes as 'a rose among thorns'. James probably came from Rheims. After studying at Paris he lived as a canon regular at St Nicolas d'Oignies. A great preacher, he helped to launch the Albigensian Crusade in 1213 and then the Fifth Crusade. His middle years were spent in the East, since he received the bishopric of Acre in 1216 and joined in the Egyptian campaign of 1218–22. The leaders of the Fifth Crusade carried out the original intention of those of the Fourth: they made for the Saracen naval bases in Egypt. Damietta was stormed after a long siege; but the crusaders could not hold it. Another crusade had failed. James returned from Overseas in 1225 and resigned his bishopric. The pope raised him to the cardinalate in 1229. He died in 1240.

81 Master Peter the Chanter is represented wearing a long clerical robe. He has a tonsure and points his fingers in the attitude of a teacher. From a manuscript produced at the German abbey of Ottobeuren on the orders of Abbot Berthold (1228–46), containing a collection of works by Master Alan of Lille, a contemporary of Peter the Chanter. *London, British Museum, MS Add. 19767, f.217r*

Colour plate IX
THE TREE OF HISTORY
(see p. 182)

A tree figure illustrating
Abbot Joachim of Fiore's
periodization of history,
probably invented by the
abbot himself. God the
Father, God the Son and
God the Holy Spirit, shown
in roundels, preside over each
of the three states of world
history. Noah, 'the righteous
man' of the Old Testament,
is shown below God the
Father as a key figure of the
first state. The two peoples,
the Jews and the gentiles, are
represented by branches,
which cross at the time of
Christ's Incarnation, only to
merge together in unity in
the third state. Joachim's
tree, like that of King
Nebuchadnezzar's dream (see
colour plate I) bears fine
foliage and fruit, which here
signify good works. In the
first state the Jewish branch
bears more fruit than the
gentile; in the second the
gentile branch, signifying
the Christian people, bears
much more than the Jewish.
In the third state, the age of
the Holy Spirit, the two
together bring forth a
wonderful abundance of
fruit. From an early
thirteenth-century
manuscript, probably from
southern Italy. *Oxford,
Corpus Christi College, MS
255A, f.4v*

An eventful career had equipped him to write contemporary history, covering both East and West. The bishop of Acre had time on his hands after the loss of Damietta. He says in his preface that 'vain tales' of Oriental kings and their exploits stirred him to write a counterblast: few Latins bothered to compose histories in modern times. He would therefore spend his leisure in writing an *Eastern* and a *Western History*. His plan, as outlined in his preface, was as follows: book one would comprise a history of Jerusalem and a description of the Holy Land; book two would deal with Western history, with special reference to the religious orders and secular clergy, ending with a section on the crusades, which would describe their religious value and usefulness; in book three he would return to the East and narrate the events which had followed the Lateran Council of 1215, that is the preaching and planning of the Fifth Crusade. It appears that he was then working on book three. However, the third book is lost; perhaps it existed only in draft. The end of book two, as we have it, differs from that proposed in the preface. The author may have changed his mind and altered the book accordingly.

James of Vitry wrote as a preacher for preachers. His description of the Holy Land was added 'to supply more abundant material for preaching'. Presumably he expected it to be used in crusading sermons and in sermons intended to kindle devotion to the Holy Places. He concludes his preface by writing that his treatise will offer an example to soldiers of Christ, strengthen faith, teach good morals, refute infidels, confound wicked men, praise good men and hold them up for imitation. It would be pointless to regret that the preacher got in the historian's way. He certainly did; but without being inspired by his duty to preach, James might not have written history at all. He might have limited himself to a saint's life, letters and sermons, which are all we have from him otherwise.

The *Eastern History* begins with a 'pocket' history of the Holy Land from Old Testament times up to the Muslim occupation. James dwells on the many ills which God has inflicted on Jerusalem. The story of the Saracen invasion leads to an account of Mohammed's life and teaching, of the Koran and of the various Muslim sectaries known to the author. Another 'pocket' history, of the crusades and the Latin kingdom and of the religious orders settled there, follows on the first. James adds a geographical description of

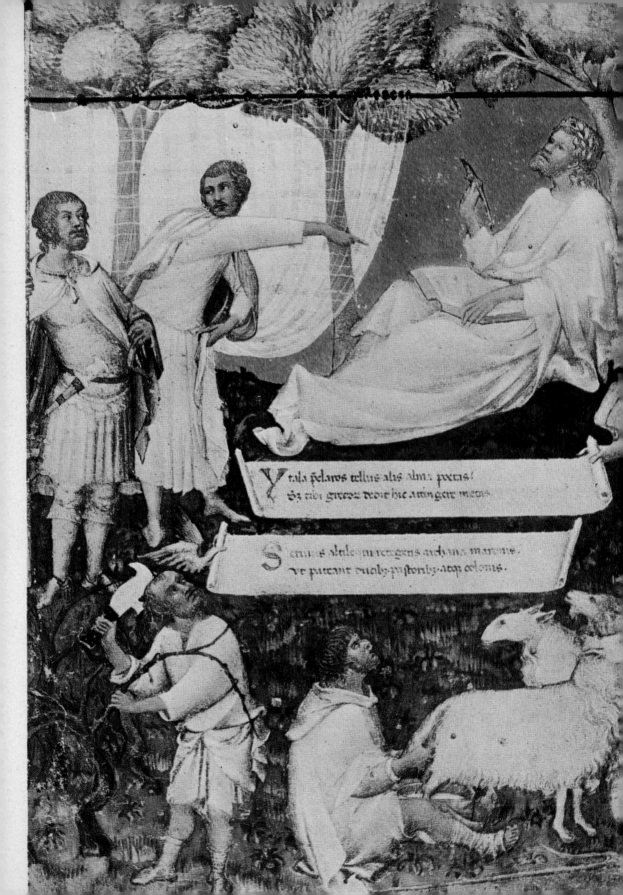

Ytala ƒelauos tellus aliis alma: poetis!
Sz tibi greeoz dedre hie attingere meris.

Serum s diduc turrengens atduna marone.
ve pateant ouibz pastonbz atap colonis.

82 Pulpit history in the making. A scholar studies at his desk and then teaches and preaches what he has learned. His lessons and sermons will be illustrated by historical *exempla*. From a thirteenth-century French manuscript of the *Bible moralisée* (see ills. 73–75). *Oxford, Bodleian Library, MS Bodl. 270b, f.125v*

Palestine. He concludes with the history of the Third Crusade and of subsequent events up to about 1210.

We do not know what books he had read for the section on Islam or how far he collected his data at first hand when he was based on Acre. He denounces Mohammed in pulpit language for the benefit of preachers who would use the *Eastern History* to stir up and warn the faithful against infidels. But he gathered some correct information about Muslim beliefs: the enquiring mind of the Paris scholar nudged the preacher in him. William of Tyre's *History* served as one of his sources for geography and history for the period it covered. James had to turn to other sources for the Third Crusade, which took place after William's death. His account of this Crusade brings out his inferiority to William of Tyre as a historian. James did not look deeply into problems of causation. Causes of disasters gave him a welcome opportunity to blame Christians for their sins, and that was all. He enjoyed himself when he rebuked the bathing habits of the decadent Latin colonists. The failure of the Third Crusade to recapture Jerusalem is ascribed solely to the

Colour plate X
A CHANGE IN ATTITUDE TO THE PAST (see pp. 192–3) The Sienese painter Simone Martini (d. 1344) illuminated the frontispiece of a copy of Virgil's poems which belonged to Petrarch and has many notes in Petrarch's handwriting. Martini has dressed Virgil in a white toga and crowned him with a laurel wreath. The warrior on the left, signifying Aeneas, wears a Roman soldier's dress. It is an attempt to lift the Roman poet out of his customary medieval setting and to present him in his proper ancient setting instead. *Milan, Biblioteca Ambrosiana, Cons. I. VIII. 74, f.1v*

quarrel between the English King Richard and the French King Philip:

They say that Saladin would have surrendered all our lands if the kings had only pretended that they would join forces to invade his territories.

James reports this doubtful hypothesis without criticism.

The *Western History* is an amalgam of genres, held together by its author's purpose as a teacher and preacher. Such unity as it has depends on its concentration on the Church. A lament for the plight of the Church in the West, described in biblical similes as 'a leafless oak tree' and 'a dried-up river', parallels the lament for her sister in the East, which opens the *Eastern History*. The devil continues to poison both head and members. The Moors in Spain, heretics in Lombardy and Provence, schismatics in Greece and false brethren everywhere have afflicted the West ever since the loss of the Holy Land. Next comes a pulpit denunciation of the sins and malpractices of men and women of all ranks, illustrated by *exempla*. One might be reading a Paris lecture course of the kind which James had heard in the Chanter's school, or a set of sermons. He paints a lurid picture of the Paris schools: the scholars form a permissive, disorderly society; the same building houses a class-room upstairs and a brothel downstairs. Light breaks through the gloom when James describes the revival of preaching, both popular and learned, fostered by Peter the Chanter, though false prophets and fake relic vendors abuse their opportunities.

The *pièce de résistance* of the *Western History* follows. James gives an account of the religious revival which marked the period from the late eleventh to the early thirteenth century. He divides the religious orders into hermits and monks, tracing each of them back to the early days of the Church, and then surveys the rise of religious reform movements. We find an almost exhaustive list of orders and of institutions such as hospitals and leper-houses, drawn up by a keen and committed observer; James belonged to the order of Canons Regular. He included with approval the *Humiliati*, an order whose members sought to lead the apostolic life as laymen. Finally he introduces us to the new mendicant orders. James had seen St Francis in person outside Damietta, when the saint went on his mission to the Saracens. The *Western History* offers us the fullest religious history of the period it covers that we have from any contemporary author.

83 St Francis preaches to the Muslims. He made a great impression on James of Vitry. Detail from an altarpiece of about 1250 attributed to Margheritone of Arezzo, in the Bardi Chapel at S. Croce, Florence.

James faced the same problem that had perplexed Otto of Freising when Otto described the religious revival of his time in his *History of the Two Cities*. How could revival occur in the evening of the last age of the world? The question mattered less to James than it did to Otto, since James took little interest in periodization. He accepted that he was living in the evening of the last age. The signs of the times persuaded him that Antichrist was just round the corner. He explained the mendicant orders' return to the Gospel precepts as a mark of divine grace: God had sent the friars to defend the faithful against Antichrist.

The bishop of Acre may have felt that he had said enough about the religious orders and that the secular clergy should have their turn. The last part of the *Western History* resembles those treatises for the instruction of priests produced in increasing numbers during the thirteenth century. The genre provides basic teaching on the structure of the Church and of her institutions and sacraments. Compilers aimed at helping the priest to minister to his parishioners. Lectures on Scripture emanating from the Chanter's circle contain the same kind of matter as the manuals for priests, arranged unsystematically, since the lecturer thought fit to mention topics arising from his text. The end of the *Western History*, like the social satire of an earlier part, stems from what James had heard when he attended classes at Paris; he probably added passages from his own sermons.

James's defects as a historian are immediately obvious. He was no analyser. What happened and what existed at the moment concerned him more than why or how things came to pass. But his careful collection of facts to put at the disposal of preachers is valuable. His *Eastern History* gives the modern scholar a good idea of what a learned man with first-hand experience knew and thought of Islam. His *Western History* tells us how the same author observed and reacted to religious reform movements.

The most ornate and fanciful specimen of pulpit history comes from Poland. Master Vincent of Cracow differs from James of Vitry in many respects, but they both aim at making history 'preachable'. Vincent left his native land to study abroad, most probably in the Paris schools. He returned to Poland before 1189. If he read theology at Paris in the 1180s he could have been influenced by Peter the Chanter and Stephen Langton. That is guessing; but it would account for Vincent's didactic purpose and his determination to play up to his audience. Paris lecture techniques are easily recognizable in his chronicle.

The returned scholar became bishop of Cracow in 1207 and attended the Lateran Council of 1215 in his capacity as bishop. He resigned his see three years later in order to become a Cistercian monk in a Polish abbey, where he died in 1223. He wrote his chronicle of Poland during these last years. Though he composed it in the cloister, his experience as a scholar and bishop sets him apart from the average monastic historian.

Master Vincent began his book with a fabulous account of the origins of the Poles. He then related Polish history up to 1202. His death prevented him from going any further. The setting of the first part of the chronicle is a dinner-table conversation between two wise old men, who discuss the history of their people. Vincent chose historical characters for his *personae*. One of them was a former bishop of Cracow and the other an archbishop of Gniezno; but the fictitious nature of the dialogue is not concealed (it is made to end in 1173, by which time the two prelates had both been dead for years). Each has his own part to play. The bishop, as befits his lower rank, has the task of telling the story, and makes only a few comments. The archbishop, his ecclesiastical superior, listens to the tale and then comments on its moral significance; he draws parallels from the history of other countries and from the Bible. The commentator points his moral lessons by adducing quotations from many different types of book; he adds proverbs, *exempla*, fables, jokes and verses of hymns. One passage of the bishop's story amuses the arch-bishop so much that he roars with laughter.

When the dialogue stops, the two old men vanish and a 'valet' or serving boy tells the story. Its commentary now takes the form of a play: personified states of mind and virtues, Joy, Sorrow, Liberty, Prudence and Moderation, discuss the meaning of what they hear. The setting will surprise a reader of Vincent's chronicle; but the prologue should have prepared his mind. It assembles a larger number of assorted quotations and mixed metaphors than any other medieval prologue to a history book that I know.

The factual value of the chronicle for the origins and early history of Poland is negligible. Having no evidence, Vincent reported legends, or possibly invented them. But he becomes a priceless source after the year 1110; then we pass from myth into history, though the scantiness of other contem-porary sources makes it hard to check his accuracy.

The chronicler had a clear purpose. He was a teacher and preacher like James of Vitry, but James addressed himself to Latin Christendom in general; Vincent addressed himself to the Poles. From this point of view he resembles William of Tyre rather than James. Vincent, like William, was a patriot. Love of his country inspired him to write its history. In both cases, the country was threatened with dismemberment: the Latin kingdom lay open to Saracen attack when William of Tyre was writing the last part of his book; Polish history went through cyclical crises. Unification under a single ruler would provoke a noble rebellion; the nobles, jealously independent, would break up the kingdom into principali-ties. The civil wars and defeat by foreign powers which followed dismemberment enabled a strong prince to gain support for establishing single rule once more. Vincent hoped that this fragile unity might be made permanent. He appealed to his readers' patriotism: 'What is done for love of one's country counts as love, not madness', he says. Solidarity is recommended as the mother of fellowship: *identitas mater est societatis*. History teaches that Poland used to be happy and strong in the good old days when the country was unified. Polish territory extended much further then than now. Present-day princes are invited to look into Vincent's chronicle as into a mirror to see their virtuous forbears, held up for imitation. As a churchman, Vincent felt bound to add that rulers would succeed all the better if they respected ecclesiastical liberties.

His chronicle won immense success. It was translated into Polish and became a textbook in Polish schools. It attracted marginal notes and commentaries, after the manner of school texts. Vincent's learned presentation suited the school-room. His chronicle, thanks to its classical allusions, had the encyclopaedic quality which the teacher needed in a set text. The teacher could refer his pupils to ancient history and myth and to classical poets as he went along. The story in itself lacked drama. Vincent could not do much with the brief annals which were all he had as sources. The decorative setting helped him out. Historians of Poland owe much to pulpit history as Vincent learned it in the Western schools. Didactic literature was a Western importation. Vincent adapted it to the needs of his people.

We may now turn from the preacher's congregations to a less specialized type of audience. The growth of an educated public led to a more widespread interest in history. Vernacular poets catered for the taste by composing histories and historical romances. The *History of William the Marshal* is a fine and well-known example of a vernacular poem on the deeds of a great English baron which serves modern historians as a primary source. Latin histories were translated into the vernacular. This gave rise to a new genre, 'history in pictures'.

Illustrated copies of histories had been few and far between before the thirteenth century. Bibles had been illustrated; but producers of histories in Latin generally contented themselves with a portrait of the author or a presentation scene to serve as a frontispiece, if they chose to illustrate the book in any way. Matthew Paris was exceptional in supplying his books with pictures. We must go to the French translations of William of Tyre's *History* if we want to find illustrations of the text. Latin and vernacular histories were presented differently. One reason for the contrast is that scholars called pictures 'the books of the laity'. Most books were written in Latin, which the layman could not understand unless he were especially well educated. He needed visual aids. It followed that a man or woman who read or heard history in the vernacular would want to see it in pictures. The need for concrete images belonged to the lay mentality. The vernacular histories which have survived are often presentation copies. A wealthy layman had a book made to order; he could afford to pay for costly illustrations. Such *de luxe* editions would be guarded as treasures and so had more chance of survival than cheaper ones.

The vogue for pictures could lead to a reversal of the functions of text and illustration. The abbey of St Mary's at York possessed a big parchment roll setting out the genealogy of the kings of England down to Edward I. It begins with the legendary story of Brutus the Trojan and his conquest of Britain. This part of the genealogy is beautifully illustrated by an artist working about 1300. The text has been reduced to several lines of writing underneath the pictures, to explain their meaning. Next the roll contains rows of 'portraits' of the kings of England with their names.

Pictures made for brighter history; but they reinforced the idea that past and present looked exactly alike. The artists who illustrated the *Great Chronicles of France* made no difference at all between the Merovingians of the fifth and sixth centuries and the Capetians of the thirteenth century when they painted costumes and court and battle scenes. The illuminator of the genealogical roll from York presents the tale of Troy in contemporary idiom. His English kings differ from one another only in their attitudes as they sit on their thrones. All wear the same type of costume as Edward I, the latest king to be depicted on the roll.

The growing interest in history inspired another type of scholar, the encyclopaedist. His task was to supply 'packaged' historical data on all periods of history known to him. A Dominican scholar called Vincent of Beauvais compiled the most extensive ever encyclopaedia of universal knowledge in about 1250. The part devoted to history, the *Speculum historiale*, alone takes up a huge folio volume in the printed edition of the *Speculum universale*. Vincent of Beauvais' history was of the world, in so far as it was known to a Westerner of the mid-thirteenth century. He refused to limit himself to the ecclesiastical and political history which formed the staple diet of medieval readers. The history of learning and of religion and mythology has its place in his *Speculum*. A whole chapter is assigned to an account of historiographers from the earliest times up to its author's own day. His interest in religion and mythology recalls James of Vitry's *Eastern* and *Western Histories*. Vincent belonged to the order of Friars Preachers, or Dominicans, and had the preacher's demand for *exempla* in mind. He differed from James in wanting to record everything that he could discover. The past appealed to him as much as the present.

THE DEVELOPMENT OF ILLUSTRATED HISTORIES
84 Overleaf, left: Latin histories were seldom illustrated. Marginal drawings were added to this copy of Orosius's *History Against the Pagans* (see pp. 44–6) as an afterthought. They show Alexander's victory at the battle of the Issus in the outer margin, and the capture of Darius's women in the lower margin. The manuscript was produced in southern Italy about 1050. *Rome, Biblioteca Apostolica Vaticana, MS Vat. lat. 3340, f.21v*

85 Overleaf, right: history in pictures. A French fourteenth-century manuscript of the *Great Chronicles of France* shows the illustration designed as an integral part of the page. King Philip II of France captures the town of Tours from King Henry II of England. *Oxford, Bodleian Library, MS Douce 217, f.260r*

175

milib; pedit. & equitu milib;
... in acie pcedit. Monebatq;
hec multitudo hostiu aduersa Ale-
xandru. maxime terrebat pau-
citas sua quamuis iam pde-
... ensis milib; hostiu aduersa
pauciorare supetabat. Non solu
non armet... pugnat. sed etia
... s; etate didicissent.
atq; cu in acie locata utriusq;
... brexisset. s; ad in-
... eos ad signu belli positos
discutienares... princeps uateris
... occiderent. Ingen-
... ueh... comnis pugnae
comitrerct. In qua ambo reges
& Alexander & dareus uul-
nerantur. Alexand... certa-
men conceps fuit. quo ad fu-
get... dareus; Deinde cedes
psecutu secuare... ibi... pe-
dicu octoginta milia & equitu
decem milia cesae car patrau.
quadraginta milia fuere;
Ex macedonu uo eccidere pedites.
... & equitu...

mulatu cruy... cenetaretur q; opi-
steppeu.; Int car pequos castion-
mare & uxor. tredes; soror. &
filiy dux dethi fuere.; Quartu se
depsione dethus cu aga o blatia
regni dimidiae partre a impetore
uissea.; Tetsio cuncea psaetu uri-
hb; socroru q; auxiliys carteca-
bellu instrutdea.; Sed du hec
dethus agiter. Alexander postue
mone. ad inuadendu psica-
claesse cu copiys mutarat.; Ipse
insyho perserent. ubi se mulas
sibi regib; cu infulys uloto occur-
tenerb; alios elegier. alios inu-
eruter. alios pdidiar.; Tyre
utbem anea qssima & flotenar-
simar... fiduciar... carthaginiensiu
sibi cognarotu obsistenat oppsita
& cepier; Sehine. ciliciar. iodu-
atq; egypetu. parnaer fusote p
uadier.; Inde ad templu iouis am-
monis pgter. ut in deereto adcep;
composreto lgnominiae sibi pa-
ceby incesti. & in frenicae adulate-
re macetys abolete.; Nae acees
sicu ad se feen ipsiuy concistem.

Cy comence le second liure des fais le
roy phelipe dieu donne

Le premier chappitre par le coment la
cite de tours et du mans fuient prises
Et puis de la mort le roy henry dangle
terre comencent les fais ·   tene
de lan · m· En lan de lincarna
cion mil c· iiij· et xc le roy af
sembla son ost au nouuel temps
et recomenca la trueue on
mois de may son ost fist condu
re vers nostent et prist le forte bernart et
quatre chasteaulx qui moult fort estoient
puis vint a la cite du mans tant fist qu la
prist par force de dens estoit le roy henry
qui sen sortit honteusement et si auoit bien
en sa compaignie c·l· cheualiers en ar
mes et tous appareilles et les chaca ius
ques au chastel de chinon qui siet en la contree de
poitou puis retourna a la cite du mans et
fist la tour miner qui moult estoit forte et
bien estarnie Quant elle fut minee si quil ny
falloit que bouter le feu ou bourdeis qui dep
estoit amasse que tout ne deffast ceulx qui
de dens estoient la rendirent Quant le roy
ot en sou demoure en le ville il sen parti et
fist son ost conduire vers la cite de tours sur
la riuiere de loire se tourneuent Quant lost
fu outre le roy monta a cheual tout seul une
lance en sa main et cheuaucha hault selon le
riuage come cil qui fut en grant de passer oult
loire comenca a regarder amont et aual pour

sauoir sil peust trouuer ne cue ne passaite en
leaue entra et aincontra a terchel et a passer le
parfont de la riuiere de la lance que il tenoit et
tousiours sicome il alloit auant mettoit en ce
tine a destre et a senestre tusques tout lost peust
passer seurement entre les enseignes ainsi
mettoit si trouua en celle maniere passaite
par ou le mesnoy onques mais plus a nul
ny seust passe et passa tout le prem a deuant
toute sa gent car la riuiere qui craint estoit
deuint petite en celle heure sicome dieu le
voult Quant le roy et tout lost furent a ilz
estoient ainsi retrautes en un moment et q
le roy estoit ia passe ilz cueillirent tantes de
tres et troussevent leur harnois en leaue se
mistrent apres le roy et passerent tous seure
ment du plus grant iusques au plus petit
Quant tous furent oultre passes les eaues
crurent arrieres en leur point et emplirent
leur chanel come deuant les bourgois de la
cite qui ce miracle virent doubterent le roy
car ils scorent bien que dieu ouurott p lui
ceste chose Adinit la bataille seint iehan bap
tandis come le roy et les barons alloient en
tour la cite pour abiser dequelle partie elle
estoit plus legiere appandre et de qt couste
len pourroit mieulx amener les enemis po
lancier aus forteresses les ribaux de lost q
a des denoient faire la premiere enuahie
quant on assault firent un assault en la cite
en la prince lestoy par eschielles monterent
sur les murs et prindrent la ville si soudaine
ment que ceulx de dedens ne sen prindrent
onques esrude le roy qui fut moult lie de
ceste aduenture reuest la cite farme et entre
sans desmarier ceulx de dedens ou dehors ses
enuirons mist dedens et puis si sen parti a
tant quant il ot demoure tant come il lui
plust Entour un iours que ces chose aui
ndrent aussi come aux octaues de la saint pere
et de saint pol morut de roy henry dengletre
ou chastel de chinon qui en sa vie ot este no
ble home et assez li fut touiours bien cheu
de toutes ses emprises et en toutes les cheu
res quil ot eues iusques au temps le roy
phelippe que dieu li mist en la bouche pour
tormter et pour courcier le sain saint thomas
archeuesque de cantorbiere quil auoit fait mar
tirer si le plus asprie diuser trent pour pou

andiafins rex gre dedit fit inā brut nonnū   crut cū clasfe ornt ad quād īnsul que vocabat leget

The *Speculum historiale* is a monument of team-work. Vincent had friar assistants to help him to collect and arrange his material. His superiors in the order tried to stop him on the reasonable ground that his gigantic enterprise cost too much money, time and labour. Vincent quietly persisted in carrying on in spite of instructions to economize. The result was the largest historical reference book of the Middle Ages. It derives from 'scissor-and-paste industry' at the highest level.

The popularity of the *Speculum* proves that it met a need for exactly that kind of book. The reader with a tough digestion could start at the beginning and plod his way through. Many more, to judge by their quotations from its pages, would dip into it or look up something that concerned them at the moment. Vincent had put an immense range of historical knowledge at the disposal of anyone who could read simple Latin and who had access to a good library. The drawback was that packaged history caused laziness, as it always will. The student has all the research done for him. He has less incentive to go to the original sources and browse among them for himself. Ideally, an encyclopaedia should serve as a guide to the original material; too often it tempts the reader to go no further. Picture histories and packaged history proved to be mixed blessings, though they spread knowledge of history over wider circles.

Here we notice a gap in thirteenth-century historiography. In all the profusion of chronicles and 'snippets' we look in vain for the old-fashioned literary history. It did not survive the early decades of the century. Various reasons suggest

86, 87 Opposite: picture history in the form of genealogy. A roll produced at the abbey of St Mary, York, about 1300 shows the arrival of Brutus in Britain, according to the legend on British origins (see p. 50). Above, he receives a wife and visits the shrine of Venus, the goddess of love. Her statue resembles images of the Virgin.

The roll goes on to illustrate the descent of English kings down to Edward I (below). The kings are portrayed in roundels. They wear the same types of costume and pose in traditional royal attitudes. *Oxford, Bodleian Library, Bodl. Roll 3*

88 The wide scope of Vincent of Beauvais' *Speculum historiale* is illustrated by a picture of the Persian King Cyrus giving orders to his troops, while a scribe sits beside him. The miniature comes at the beginning of book iv in a French fourteenth-century copy. *Oxford, Merton College, MS 2.7–10*

themselves to explain why it disappeared. There had been an element of chance in the marriage between talent and opportunity. We owe a lot of historical writing to frustrated ambition. If William of Tyre had realized his wish to become patriarch of Jerusalem, or Gerald of Wales his lifelong ambition to become archbishop of St David's, they would have left us less history. If John of Salisbury had not been driven into exile, he might never have written up his *Memoirs of the Papal Court*.

But chance and personalities are insufficient explanations. Academic developments militated against literary history. The genre 'literary history' was a child of rhetoric as taught in the Arts course. The study of rhetoric declined in the late twelfth century, and with it the means to gain a sound classical education. Students turned away from grammar and rhetoric to logic and dialectic. They skimmed over their Latin grammar and read fewer literary texts in their hurry to learn logic, natural science and philosophy. The new translations of Aristotle which were becoming available acted as a magnet in the schools.

The result was that thirteenth-century historiographers did not care to write elegant Latin. That in itself need not have lessened their competence as historians. On the contrary, the use of an unclassical style gave them freedom to express their thoughts more spontaneously. But style and content went together. Historiographers impoverished themselves when they read classical histories in extracts, as it was tempting to do, instead of soaking themselves in the originals. The ancient historians offered models of structure as well as rules of style: they taught their imitators to reflect on causation. The literary history with its classical background was more conducive to reflection than the chronicle.

To find a deeper reason for the absence of literary history we have to look at the intellectual trends of the thirteenth century. The schoolmen did not write history even in their spare time. Aristotle, their philosopher, gave them no guidance in this field. His many works contain historical allusions in plenty and he used a historical approach to problems that interested him; but he did not write any history. Theologians who studied in the schools continued to think of history as the history of salvation. As such it formed a background to their theology. Otherwise they made history serve practical ends: it had entertainment value as recreation; it provided preachers with *exempla*; it supplied precedents which could be cited in disputes on privilege and status. Thirteenth-century schoolmen put their creative effort into the discussion of problems concerning man as he is. They asked: 'What is man like in himself? What are his relations with his fellow-men? What is his relationship to God?' The answers to these questions depended less on what men had done in the past than on what they were doing now and on what the schoolmen thought they ought to do. Clio lost her appeal.

The philosopher Peter of Abano made a disparaging comment on the Muse in his *Exposition of Aristotle's Problems*, published at Padua in 1310. As a scientist Peter excluded history from scientific knowledge. His reason was that the historian, unlike the scientist, could not proceed from cause to effect or from effect to cause by inductive and deductive reasoning. Hence the composition of histories struck Peter as 'merely a laborious and pointless piling up of examples'. We cannot know what a Paris doctor of the thirteenth century would have thought of this sneer at history; it seems likely, though, that he would have regarded chroniclers as his intellectual inferiors. Master William of Puylaurens, describing the Albigensian crusade, gives a tantalizing taste of what a man trained in the schools and not obsessed by preaching could achieve when he chose to write history; but he stands alone.

Historiography met a supreme challenge just when there was no Otto of Freising to deal with it. The Calabrian abbot Joachim of Fiore (d. 1202) put forward a new time scheme and a new pattern of history. Joachim was not a historian, but a commentator on Scripture, a religious reformer and a prophet. Nevertheless, his ideas had deep implications for anyone who reflected on historical periodization. The Calabrian abbot developed the traditional Christian view that the Old Testament prefigured and foreshadowed the New. There were two dispensations in the history of man's salvation; Joachim held to that. But he went on to predict a third age in religious history. The second dispensation included a third age. The Old Testament represented the age of God the Father, the New Testament that of God the Son; the third age would be the age of the Holy Spirit, proceeding from the Father and the Son. Joachim believed that mankind was standing on the threshold of this third age; he could see the signs of what was coming.

He worked out correspondences between the ages and allowed for overlapping between them. The Old Testament corresponded to the Order of Wedlock, since the patriarchs of Israel had married, according to God's plan to people the earth. The New Testament corresponded to the Order of Clerks. The third age would be the age of monks. The hermits of the Old Testament and St John the Baptist had prepared the way for the second age. St Benedict, founder of Western monasticism, prepared the way for the monks who would characterize the third age of the world. The new order always emerged from the womb of the old. The monks of the third age would be holier and more spiritual than their predecessors. The age of the Holy Spirit would begin with the coming of a new Elias. Then twelve holy men would appear, corresponding to the twelve apostles of the Gospel. Joachim altered the traditional order by putting the coming of the first Antichrist, who would bring trials and tribulations to the faithful, before the last age. The first Antichrist would come and suffer defeat before the reign of the Holy Spirit could be established. The third age, when the Holy Spirit would reign, would last until the coming of the second Antichrist and Doomsday. Religion would be perfected in the third age and an angelic pope would rule the Church.

Pat on the heels of Joachim's prophecies came the new orders of mendicant friars. St Francis and his companions fitted into the picture of the new Elias and his twelve holy men. The emperor Frederick II fell neatly into the role of the first Antichrist. If Joachim's predictions were about to be fulfilled, then the third age must be dawning. The abbot's disciples carried his conclusions further than he would have dreamed. Works falsely ascribed to him circulated. Interest showed itself in the production of 'books of figures', where the Joachist outline of history and of its future course were shown in the form of trees with branches and captions to explain what they meant. Some of the figures go back to the early days of Joachism; others develop the abbot's ideas on extraordinary lines. Joachism spread like wildfire. Its extremist forms led to heresy, but papal condemnations failed to quench the flame. Its influence on religious prophecy lasted into the seventeenth century.

Joachim's vision of the sweep of history, in contrast to the traditional view handed down by St Augustine and Orosius, was dynamic rather than static. Joachim kept their idea that one age led up to the following age; but he opened up a prospect of a new and better era, which he inserted between the first and second coming of Antichrist. The troubles in store for us at Antichrist's first coming were to be a prelude to the reign of the Holy Spirit in this world.

The new pattern suggested by Joachim presented historiographers with an opportunity to revise their views on time schemes. He challenged them to look for signs of progress instead of remaining bogged down in the old age of the world. True, Joachim postulated religious progress only; but religious and secular history hung together. It should have been possible to pick up the threads of optimism to be found in the works of Hugh of St Victor and other twelfth-century writers. Historiographers failed to respond. The story of the abbot and his disciples and of their prophecies appealed to chroniclers as news items. They report the prophecies with varying degrees of scepticism and credulity. Salimbene went through a Joachist phase, only to be disillusioned when Frederick II did not come up to scratch as Antichrist: Frederick's death in 1250 brought little change in the world. Salimbene had no idea of planning his chronicle according to the time scheme of Joachim's three ages. Thirteenth-century chroniclers did not attempt to test the new periodization in order to decide whether it applied to their material. If anyone tested and rejected it as a useful tool to the historian, he did so in silence.

The contrast between historiographers on the one hand, and theologians and prophets on the other, is difficult to explain. Were chroniclers afraid of falling into heresy? Fear of heresy had small effect on speculation in the universities. Why should chroniclers have been especially nervous? Perhaps they refrained from speculating on the course of universal history out of common sense. Perhaps they had too little interest in ideas. Perhaps their silence is another reflection of their intellectual inferiority vis-à-vis the schoolmen. For whatever reason, they fought shy of Joachism, leaving others to discuss its merits or to refute it, as the case might be.

A modern historian may warm to this 'no nonsense' attitude on the part of thirteenth-century historiographers. We tend to regard 'prophetic history' as a pitfall, or a blind alley at best. But Joachim challenged historiographers to revise their traditional time schemes. Perhaps they showed a wise caution in keeping to tradition. In any case, they preferred caution to enterprise. The thirteenth century lacked a 'reflective' historian.

Conclusions

We can now consider the question, why did anyone write history when it brought him no financial or professional reward for his pains? The closest parallel to the modern professional historian in the Middle Ages seems to be the court entertainer, who composed and recited 'songs' on ·historical topics; he earned his living by doing so; but his 'songs' fall outside the most serious kind of historiography. It will help to answer the question if we begin at the consumers' end and ask, not why history was written, but why it was needed.

Isidore said in his *Etymologies* that record-keeping was 'useful'. That was true: rulers and corporate bodies, such as town councils and religious houses, needed to have records kept for purposes of reference and to substantiate their political and legal claims. Chronicles served as record books. Pleasure and pride in the past added to the desire to have events recorded. Members of a family or of an institution took an interest in the story of their origins and of their ancestors. The historian of a family, episcopal see, abbey, town or people expected to find interested readers or hearers. Belonging to the group himself, he would identify with his theme and his audience. It was his honour and his duty to satisfy their demands. The group might be larger or smaller. It could comprise a whole country: William of Tyre and Vincent of Cracow wrote expressly from motives of patriotism, to instruct their compatriots. If the tale were a sad one, the writer could give vent to his people's grief: the anonymous *Life of Henry IV* is a dirge for the decline of the empire; the anonymous part of the *Song of the Albigensian Crusade* is a lament for the plight of the Midi.

History also served for recreation, though this is not stated in the *Etymologies*. Hunting was the sport of kings; listening to stories was their pastime. Natural entertainers perform in all ages. We have seen them at work, from the tenth-century *salon* historians to William of Tyre amusing King Amalric and William of Tudela at the court of Count

Baldwin. A churchman could salve his conscience by pointing to the exemplarist value of history. It pertained to his office to instruct the laity: history provided a happy means to a good end. Indeed it could convey a dire warning: William of Puylaurens wrote his chronicle to show how the sins of his people had led to disaster. An element of sheer curiosity also entered into the search for news items and more rarely into the scholarly investigation of antiquities.

To choose history rather than chronicle involved thought and labour. The historian had to watch his style. He deliberately avoided a year-by-year framework, which meant that he had to plan his presentation more carefully. Yet many authors took the trouble to write history. The choice in itself marked the historian as a classicist. Desire to emulate the ancients inspired some of the best writers of the Middle Ages from the ninth to the twelfth centuries, and not least the historians. The cult of letters distinguished civilized men from mere brutes. History ranked high by ancient standards as a dignified branch of literature. 'Emulation' is a better term than 'imitation' to describe the medieval historian's attitude. His story deserved the honour of elegant narrative as much as Caesar's or Sallust's. He paid homage to his theme by adapting their techniques and language to suit his material.

The propaganda motive dominated medieval historiography, as it had Roman. Biographies show it in its crudest form: a royal biography was a propaganda piece by definition. The biographer might work to order, as the Anonymous of St Omer did for Emma in her lifetime, or he might praise the ruler after his death at the request of friends or heirs. Apart from conventional eulogy, he stressed whichever aspect of the ruler appealed to him as a lay noble or as monk or prelate. Histories, chronicles and memoirs carry propaganda of an equally obvious or at least perceptible kind. Today the word propaganda implies an intention to mislead. Originally, during the Counter Reformation, it meant 'the propagation of the faith'. We are using the word in this second sense when we describe medieval historiography as 'propagandist'. Writers often had a religious purpose uppermost in their minds, and said so. The more secular-minded advertised a cause which was dear to their hearts; thus Caffaro wrote for Genoa and Villehardouin for his fellow-crusaders. Interest and idealism shade into each other. It is always hard to separate them, and hardest of all in medieval historiography. Our authors normally wrote on behalf of an institution or fellowship. The propagandist, unless he is paid, has a personal stake in swaying public opinion. In the Middle Ages his personal interest merged into his *esprit de corps*.

One unshakable belief supported all these motives. What happened mattered and ought to be remembered. 'Despise the world and its vanities', said the preacher; 'save them from oblivion', said the scholar, who was often the same as the preacher. Historiographers acted on the second precept.

It is more difficult to estimate their achievement than to explain why they wrote. C. H. Haskins, a great medievalist, warns us that 'the historian has no business to award prizes for modernity'. A judge must know the rules of the game; that is certain. We should not blame a chronicler for not writing history, nor look in a biography for the facts and dates that we expect to find in a chronicle. But we can try to measure the distance between medieval and modern standards. There are no absolute standards in historiography; they change all the time. We can only use those which we apply to ourselves nowadays. In one respect the ideal has not changed: the historiographer must tell the truth. But how to find it? Dearth of research tools, absence of perspective and blind faith in the value of eyewitness accounts – all frustrated the medieval historiographer in his enquiries. On the question of bias, today we try to check our personal prejudices by awareness of them and by scrupulous honesty in our use of evidence. In that we score over our medieval forerunners, and in that only. To accuse them of bias would be like throwing stones in glass houses. No one can write history without having ideas about what comes into it; and ideas imply bias. What we can ask is whether an author tries to be objective. We exclude supernatural agencies as an element in causation, except in so far as belief in the supernatural has been a factor in the making of history. But the historiographer has to write of the world as he knows it. The medieval historiographer wrote of a world which included supernatural agents. Even so, he never regarded men as mere puppets. It is possible to ask of him: how far does he leave all the work to God and the devil and how far does he consider human or natural causes?

The fairest way to measure achievement is to take the point of departure. What did medieval historiographers make of their sources? They inherited a jumble of rules, models and definitions. The Romans left them guidelines which, although twisted, were indispensable to the writing of contemporary or near contemporary history. The Jewish-Christian legacy taught them to attempt universal history. This heritage put man at the centre of a cosmic drama, the history of salvation: time began with Genesis and would end at Doomsday. The historiographer therefore had to embrace the 'universe', and the whole of recorded history. It sounds a tall order; but the territory to be covered and the records of its history were limited. His task was easier than one might suppose, since Isidore told him that to write pre-contemporary history consisted of copying from earlier sources; it was mere compilation. Orosius handed down a standard model of universal history or chronicle, arranged according to the time scheme of the six ages of the world and the four world monarchies. The Roman legacy of historical monograph, biographies and eulogies fitted into the wider framework as permitted alternatives. Eusebius provided a model of Church history and Orosius presented profane history from the point of view of the Church historian. For profane history as such the classical models gave the only guidance available. Attempts were made to keep the two kinds separate; but they foundered. Ecclesiastical and secular history mingled increasingly as the Church came to play a greater part in secular life and to monopolize letters. Learned churchmen knew both their Latin classics and their Bible and used them as ingredients in varying degrees when they turned to historiography.

The mixed inheritance carried dangers. Medieval writers leaned too heavily on their authorities. Ancient and biblical characters get in the way of the story. The historiographer appropriated them and costumed them, or made his contemporaries use their language. It comes as a relief to the modern reader when they stay in the background or disappear from the scene. The Orosian periodization was accepted as a dogma and proved to be an incubus. The span of the four world monarchies sometimes provoked questions; more often it was ignored. No historiographer replaced it by any other form of periodization. Joachim of Fiore proposed a new time scheme and a new outlook on history. Historiographers left the stone unturned, either because they dared not break with tradition or because historical speculation did not appeal to them.

Men with a speculative bent made straight for the schools – monastic, cathedral or university. Otto of Freising stands alone as a scholar-historian who had ideas about history and who tested them in the light of his experience. The same reluctance to question tradition comes out in the attitude to barbarian history. Folk legends and learned inventions on the origins of peoples came down as part of the stock-in-trade. Medieval writers generally imitated instead of criticizing these fake origins; new fakes proliferated. William of Malmesbury and William of Newburgh are both famous for their scepticism on the subject of romances about early British history. The fame of these romances testifies to the general level of credulity. It was not a matter of inertia in this case, as it was in the acceptance of the Orosian time scheme. Rather, the attitude was 'me too!' Respectable peoples and towns had to have ancient or biblical ancestors, or preferably both, just as sees and abbeys often had legendary foundation stories. Local pride led to the study of history, but also to the invention of fake history.

These are small specks on the bubbling creativeness of medieval historiography. We have *salon* history, religious history of many kinds, local history, court history, pulpit history, 'country party' history, war history, colonial history, nostalgic history and even reflective history. A rich assortment of genres came down as part of the medieval inheritance, stretching from Sallust's monographs to the *Popes' Book* and Paul the Deacon's *History of Metz*. Historiographers showed a talent for adapting an old genre to new uses. The writer of a saint's life and passion saw himself as continuing the Gospel. The New Testament received some unlikely supplements in Wipo's *Life* of the tough emperor Conrad II and in the anonymous *Deeds of the Franks*. A real breakthrough came in portraiture. Suetonius' static portraits of rulers began to take on life. Adam of Bremen describes an archbishop turning into a megalomaniac. Jocelyn of Brakelonde shows how Samson's office as abbot brought out his masterful character. William of Malmesbury points to the connection between King Stephen's character and the events of his reign. Stephen was on the wrong side anyway, from William's point of view; but his defects prevented him from winning in the civil war as long as William lived to record its history. William of Tyre notes how the characters of the kings of Jerusalem affected the defence of their kingdom.

Personal memoirs are the *forte* of medieval historiography, as we have seen. In modern times memoirs have often taken the form of autobiography. This was exceptional in the Middle Ages. Guibert of Nogent, untypical and original,

Abelard and Gerald of Wales made the closest approaches to autobiography in the period between 800 and 1300. Introspection took other forms, such as prayers or meditations. The memoir writer described his experiences as a member of a group instead of focusing on his 'self': he observed and participated, but did not put himself forward in his own right. We have memoirs in pure form in Liudprand's account of his embassy to Constantinople and in the stories of Galbert of Bruges and of Geoffrey of Villehardouin; and memoirs form part of many other genres of historiography, often the best part. The reporter escaped from the temptation to imitate and he had an impetus to write freshly and directly.

Still, memoirs are not history. The historian must try to find connections between the events he describes; he must ask 'why?' as well as 'what?' and 'how?'. The best one can say for medieval historians is that they responded to shock treatment. Questions asked themselves. The Investiture Contest, the rise of towns, the growth of bureaucracy, border warfare, the crusades and the spread of heresy all posed problems. Why did Henry IV fail as an emperor? Why did the Saxon freedom fighters fail? Why the slaughter at Bruges? Was Henry II justified in restricting ecclesiastical liberties in the interests of law and order? Why did the heathen Slavs and the Irish resist for so long? Why did the kingdom of Jerusalem decline? Why did heresy spread in the Midi? These were non-questions to a disciple of Orosius. For him, history boiled down to the story of human misery; why pick on a particular episode as extraordinary? But historians minded about particular episodes which concerned them. They looked for particular causes. The old answers lay ready to hand: God punishes sin; his ways are inscrutable; Fortune turns her wheel; modern luxury softens morals and leads to defeat. Such answers struck some historians as inadequate: they left too much unexplained. The more thoughtful writers came up with shrewd, commonsense reasons. Ralph of Diss decided that some questions were better left alone; so he found an escape route by putting his data in separate compartments. At least he saw his problem.

Discernment of motive is still one of the most elusive problems which face the historian. We find it difficult enough to analyse our own. When we tackle the motives of a character in history we have no evidence, unless he or his associates stated them, and that may well have been propaganda. All we can safely say is that he had an interest in taking a certain course; but he may have had quite a different notion of where his interests lay; he may even have preferred to do what he thought was his duty; he may have been plain stupid. The problem of motive fascinated medieval historians. Guibert of Nogent in his history of the First Crusade underlined the difficulty of establishing human motives. As the author of an autobiography, he had more experience of introspection than most historiographers. Others rushed in where he feared to tread. Again, however, shrewd common sense inspired their guesses at motives for action. It was normal to contrast what a person gave out as his reason for acting in a certain way to what he was really aiming at. Historiographers on the whole did not err on the side of being 'starry-eyed'. They were too cynical if anything: 'suspect the worst.'

Complete objectivity is impossible to achieve at all times. Medieval historiographers had an extra handicap; their best efforts went into writing contemporary or near contemporary history, in which partiality is built into the narrative. But we do find brave attempts to stand outside and to see more than one viewpoint. Adam of Bremen and Helmold tried to understand the Slavs; John of Salisbury lent over backward to be fair to both St Bernard and Gilbert of la Porrée; William of Puylaurens succeeded in putting the southerners' point of view on heresy, explaining why it spread and why it was not resisted, without excusing the heretics. Going back to the ninth century, we find Walafrid Strabo criticizing the historian Thegan for his partiality to Louis the Pious. Signs of a wish to be objective show through medieval historiography in spite of its usually propagandist purpose. The Middle Ages produced brilliant propagandists. Surprisingly, there was room for historians too.

Finally, we expect a historian to rely on evidence and to show his hand. Footnotes are a modern invention, but it was possible to quote documentary evidence and to copy inscriptions. Suetonius did so; Eusebius made it part of the technique of writing Church history. Secular and Church history intermingled and there was cross-fertilization. The tyranny of ancient biography and of medieval hagiography tended to keep documentary evidence out of *Lives* of rulers and saints, though it did creep into them during the twelfth century. Monographs, histories and chronicles, on the other hand, increasingly supply copies of letters, charters, treaties and laws. Historiographers sometimes had a propagandist reason for inserting them; others saw documents as an integral part of the story they had to tell. They sacrificed literary elegance to their duty to be informative.

We can watch modern historiography developing gradually in the Middle Ages. Our predecessors started from a small residue of ancient histories. Many have been lost; but we have more than were obtainable in the Middle Ages. Medieval historiographers made full and imaginative use of their legacy such as it was. Sometimes it acted as a crutch; the more adventurous put it aside and walk on their own feet. This is especially true of lay writers; these had to be self-sufficient and original when book learning had become a privilege of clergy.

The history of an art or science never registers steady progress. There are always lapses, whatever standard we take as our measuring-rod. Historiography almost disappeared in the decades about 900. History as distinct from chronicle lapsed again in the thirteenth century. The twelfth-century Latin historians remained unsurpassed in the thirteenth. One can browse with pleasure in thirteenth-century chronicles, as well as reading them as source material; but one misses any awareness of history's special function. These writers are shallow compared with William of Malmesbury, Otto of Freising or William of Tyre.

The turn of the century makes a convenient stopping place. The years after 1300 saw new developments in the writing of history and new ideas about how it should be written. Monks and clerks continued to produce histories and chronicles in Latin. Secular clerks were especially busy in England. But the fourteenth century is more famous for its vernacular chroniclers. The lay historian, a soldier or a city official, comes into the foreground. He tells of events which he has seen and taken part in. We have Joinville's *Life of St Louis*, the chronicle of the Catalan general Ramon Muntaner, the Anglo-Norman *Scalachronicon*, Froissart's chronicles of the Anglo-French wars and the Villani chronicles of Florence, to mention only a few outstanding names. The German *Stadtchronik*, or town chronicle, became a major source for imperial history.

Learned Latin historiography revived. A schoolman turned to history without thinking it beneath his dignity as an academic. The Oxford Dominican friar Nicholas Trevet wrote extensively in both Latin and French. He was a polymath and history was one of his many interests. Livy came into fashion as an author. His history of Rome had been

89 A genuine sense of history, of the past as different from the present, begins to appear in the work of Giotto. In his fresco of the Flagellation, painted in the Arena Chapel at Padua about 1305, Pontius Pilate is for the first time an entirely non-medieval figure. No longer bearded and robed in dateless draperies, he is clearly a Roman, distinguished from the Jews around him. His massive head is garlanded, and his robe bears the imperial eagle in gold.

known in the earlier period, but he was little read. Now he became a favourite among the élite. Trevet led the way at Oxford at the turn of the century in his study of Livy. His commentary on Livy's *History* was sought after and read at the papal court at Avignon. The vogue reflected a serious interest in ancient history and antiquities.

The achievements of twelfth-century historians grew out of their loving study of the Latin classics, as we have seen. The early fourteenth-century revival of classical studies had the same stimulating effect on historians. A group of scholars at Padua, Livy's birthplace, took the Roman writer to themselves. They did not merely imitate his classical style. The bewildering changes in Italian history from ancient times up to their own day led them to reflect on problems of periodization. The Paduan 'prehumanists', as the group is now called, experimented with new genres and new time schemes. Albertino Mussato was probably the first historian since Otto of Freising to write 'reflective history'. He had a more secular and local approach to his subject than Otto; but they both felt the same urge to put the untidy facts of history into an intelligible order. Their originality, if nothing else, makes a link between the German Cistercian bishop and the Paduan citizen.

More decisive than these experiments, brave though they were, is the change in men's attitude to the past. The student of medieval historiography gets used to living in an intellectual world in which he can converse with Adam and Eve or Julius Caesar or Charlemagne as though they were neighbours. As soon as we know our historian, we know how he will imagine the past; it will look like the present. In the fourteenth century the sense of continuity snapped. It was no longer a question of decline from a better age. An old man in his last years can still identify with the boy that he used to be. Now, suddenly, it was as though the old man had lost his memory and recovered to find himself in a prison or madhouse. Petrarch saw that a gulf separated ancient culture from the chivalry and scholasticism of his time. Contemporary institutions struck him as 'barbarous'. He announced his discovery with the voice of genius; but it was part of a general stock-taking. To good Catholics as well as to heretics the fourteenth-century Church looked more like Babylon than the primitive community of the apostles. In ecclesiastical history as in secular the contrast between past and present loomed too large to admit of any continuous development.

The humanists did not 'rediscover the past'. It belonged to the medieval inheritance from antiquity. What they did was to discover the past *as* past. History was seen in perspective, not as a painting on a flat surface. The humanists' perspective looks faulty today. Their judgments on the past were distorted. But the attempt at perspective of any kind makes all the difference to the presentation of history. In that sense, modern historiography begins in the fourteenth century.

The new vision affected the writing of history slowly and partially. As often happens, the men who had new ideas about history did not write it, and history was left to the conservatives. We have seen that theologians and canon lawyers showed more awareness of the possibility of change for the better than did historiographers. So it was in the fourteenth century. Humanists and reformers showed more awareness of the gap between past and present than did historiographers, with few exceptions. A reader fresh from studying thirteenth-century chronicles will feel quite at home when he turns to chroniclers in the fourteenth century; he will find the same methods and the same outlook on the past. Nevertheless, he needs to watch his step and prepare himself for a change of climate. It would not do to omit Darwin's *Origin of Species* from a history of ideas, just because most of Darwin's contemporaries still believed that God created man in paradise. Even if the old conventions and time schemes lingered on in late medieval historiography, the modern reader knows that the *avant garde* had other views on history. The older notions begin to seem dull and stale. They lasted for a millennium, which is a long time in the history of ideas.

Bibliography

CHAPTERS 1–4
General and introductory reading
R. G. Collingwood, *The Idea of History* (Oxford, 1946)
B. Croce, *Theory and History of Historiography*, trans. D. Ainslie
  (London, 1921)
H. Grundmann, 'Geschichtsschreibung im Mittelalter', *Deutsche
  Philologie im Aufriss*, ed. W. Stammer, xxvi (1952–9), 1273–1335
B. M. Lacroix, 'The Notion of History in Early Medieval Historians',
  Mediaeval Studies, x (Toronto, 1948), 219–23; and *L'Historien au
  moyen âge*, Montreal and Paris 1971
A. Momigliano, 'Pagan and Christian Historiography in the Fourth
  Century A.D.', *The Conflict between Paganism and Christianity in the
  Fourth Century*, ed. A. Momigliano (Oxford, 1963), 79–99
J. T. Shotwell, *The History of History*, i (New York, 1939), 255–377
B. Smalley, 'Sallust in the Middle Ages', *Classical Influences on European
  Culture, A.D. 500–1500*, ed. R. R. Bolgar (Cambridge, 1971)
R. W. Southern, 'Aspects of the European Tradition of Historical
  Writing. 1. The Classical Tradition from Einhard to Geoffrey of
  Monmouth'; '2. Hugh of St Victor and the Idea of Historical
  Development'; '3. History as Prophecy', *Transactions of the Royal
  Historical Society*, 5th series, xx–xxii (1970–72). To be completed by
  'The Sense of the Past', forthcoming
J. W. Thompson and B. J. Holm, *A History of Historical Writing*, 2 vol.
  (New York, 1942, reprint, 1967)

Texts in translation
Latin Historians and *Latin Biography*, ed. T. A. Dorey (London, 1966,
  1967)
English Historical Documents, ed. D. C. Douglas, i–iii (from 1955), gives
  many excerpts from English and Anglo-Norman historians and
  chroniclers with introductions. The best known are translated in full
  in Bohn's Antiquarian Library

CHAPTERS 5 AND 6
La Storiografia Altomedievale (Settimane di Studio del Centro Italiano di
  Studio sull'Alto Medioevo, xvii, 2 vol., Spoleto, 1970) has papers in
  English, French, German, Italian and Spanish on early medieval
  historiography, up to the 11th century
D. A. Bullough, '*Europae Pater:* Charlemagne and his achievement in
  the light of recent scholarship', *English Historical Review*, lxxxv
  (1970), 59–105
J. Leclercq, 'Monastic historiography from Leo IX to Callistus II',
  Studia Monastica, xii (1970), 57–86

Christopher Brooke, *The Twelfth Century Renaissance* (London, 1969)
R. W. Southern, *Medieval Humanism and Other Studies* (Oxford, 1970)
C. Morris, *The Discovery of the Individual 1050–1200* (London, 1972)
V. H. Galbraith, *Historical Research in Medieval England* (London, 1951)
H. Farmer, 'William of Malmesbury's Life and Works', *Journal of Ecclesiastical History*, xiii (1962), 39–54

Texts in translation
Einhard, *The Life of Charlemagne*, trans. L. Thorpe (London, 1970)
Carolingian Chronicles: Royal Frankish Annals and Knithard's Histories, trans. B. W. Scholz and B. Rogers (Michigan, 1970)
Imperial Lives and Letters of the Eleventh Century, trans. T. E. Mommsen and K. F. Morrison (Records of Civilization, New York, 1962)
Helgaud de Fleury, *Vie de Robert le Pieux*, ed. and trans. (French) R.-H. Bautier and G. Labory (Sources d'histoire médiévale, Paris, 1965)
Suger, *Vie de Louis VI le Gros*, ed. and trans. (French) H. Waquet (Classiques de l'histoire de France au Moyen âge, Paris, 1929)
Encomium Emmae Reginae, ed. and trans. Alistair Campbell (Camden 3rd series, lxxii, London, 1949)
The Works of Liudprand of Cremona, trans. F. A. Wright (London, 1930)
Richer, *Histoire de France 888–995*, ed. and trans. (French) R. Latouche (Classiques de l'histoire de France au Moyen âge, Paris, 1930–67)
The Anglo-Saxon Chronicle, a revised translation, ed. D. Whitelock (London, 1961)
The Ecclesiastical History of Orderic Vitalis, ed. and trans. M. Chibnall (Oxford, 1969–72)
The Historia Novella of William of Malmesbury, ed. and trans. K. R. Potter (London, 1955)

CHAPTER 7
A. D. von den Brincken, *Studien zur lateinischen Weltchronistik bis in das Zeitalter Otto von Freisings* (Düsseldorf, 1957)

Texts in translation
Otto of Freising, *The Two Cities*, trans. C. C. Mierow (Records of Civilization, New York, 1928)
The Deeds of Frederick Barbarossa by Otto of Freising and his Continuator Rahewin, trans. C. C. Mierow (Records of Civilization, New York, 1953)

CHAPTER 8
D. M. Stenton, 'Roger of Howden and *Benedict*', *English Historical Review*, lxviii (1953), 574–82
A History of St Paul's Cathedral and the Men associated with it, ed. W. R. Matthews and W. M. Atkins (London, 1957)
For Caffaro's Genoa, see below, chapter 9 (Boase)

Texts in translation
The Murder of Charles the Good by Galbert of Bruges, trans. J. B. Ross (Records of Civilization, New York, 1960)
John of Salisbury's Memoirs of the Papal Court, ed. and trans. M. Chibnall (London, 1956)

CHAPTER 9

A. P. Vlasto, *The Entry of the Slavs into Christendom* (Cambridge, 1970)

T. S. R. Boase, *Kingdoms and Strongholds of the Crusaders* (London, 1971) gives a bibliography which is also useful for Caffaro's Genoa (see chapter 8)

A. C. Krey, 'William of Tyre', *Speculum*, xvi (1941), 149–66

R. B. C. Huygens, 'Guillaume de Tyr étudiant. Un chapitre de son *Histoire* retrouvé', *Latomus*, xxi (1962), 811–29

B. M. Lacroix, 'Guillaume de Tyr. Unité et diversité dans la tradition latine', *Etudes d'histoire littéraire et doctrinale*, 4th series (Paris, 1968), 201–15

C. Morris, 'Villehardouin and the Conquest of Constantinople', *History*, liii (1968), 24–34

P. Belperron, *La Croisade contre les Albigeois et l'union du Languedoc à la France (1209–1249)* (Paris, 1946)

R. I. Moore, 'The Origins of Medieval Heresy', *History*, lv (1970), 21–36

Texts in translation

Adam of Bremen, *History of the Archbishops of Hamburg-Bremen*, trans. F. J. Tschan (Records of Civilization, New York, 1959)

Helmold, *The Chronicle of the Slavs*, trans. F. J. Tschan (Records of Civilization, New York, 1935)

J. J. O'Meara and A. B. Scott are preparing a new edition and translation of Gerald of Wales, *De expugnatione Hiberniae*; meanwhile on Gerald of Wales see the first version of his *Topographia*, trans. J. J. O'Meara (Dundalk, 1951)

Anonymous, *Deeds of the Franks*, ed. and trans. Rosalind Hill (London, 1962)

William of Tyre, *A History of deeds done beyond the sea*, trans. E. A. Babcock and A. C. Krey (Records of Civilization, New York, 1943)

Chronicles of the Crusades. Histoire de Saint Louis. La Conquête de Constantinople, trans. M. R. B. Shaw (London, 1967)

Pierre des Vaux de Cernai, *Histoire Albigeoise*, trans. (French) P. Guébin and H. Maisonneuve (Paris, 1951)

Chanson de la Croisade Albigeoise, trans. (French from Provençal) E. Martin-Chabot (Classiques de l'histoire de France au Moyen âge, Paris, 1931–61)

Chronique de Guillaume de Puy Laurens contenant l'histoire de l'expédition contre les Albigeois, trans. (French) C. Lagarde (Béziers, 1864)

CHAPTER 10

R. Brentano, *Two Churches: England and Italy in the Thirteenth Century* (Princeton, 1968), 306–45, compares Matthew Paris and Salimbene as chroniclers and gives bibliography

P. David, *Les Sources de l'histoire de Pologne* (Paris, 1934), 56–72, gives an account of Vincent of Cracow

B. L. Ullman, 'A Project for a New Edition of Vincent of Beauvais', *Speculum*, viii (1933), 312–26

N. G. Siraisi, 'The *Expositio Problematum Aristotelis* of Peter of Abano', *Isis*, lxi (1970), 321–39

M. E. Reeves, *The Influence of Prophecy in the Later Middle Ages* (Oxford, 1970)

Texts

The Chronicle of Jocelin of Brakelond concerning the acts of Samson, ed. and trans. H. E. Butler (London, 1949)

Matthew Paris's English History, trans. J. A. Giles (London, 1852–4)

Thomas of Eccleston and Jordan of Giano, trans. E. Gurney Salter (London, 1926)

Grandes chroniques de la France, ed. J. Viard (Paris, 1920–34)

CHAPTER 11

B. Smalley, *English Friars and Antiquity in the Early Fourteenth Century* (Oxford, 1960), chapter 12

Peter Burke, *The Renaissance Sense of the Past* (London, 1969)

D. R. Kelley, *Foundations of Modern Historical Scholarship: Language, Law and History in the French Renaissance* (New York and London, 1970)

Texts

For original texts see A. Potthast, *Bibliotheca historica medii aevi* (Berlin, 1895–6). A new edition of Potthast is in progress, *Repertorium fontium historiae medii aevi* (Rome, 1962–70)

ACKNOWLEDGMENTS

Most of the photographs from which reproductions have been made were supplied by the institutions mentioned in the captions in italic type. The publishers would also like to thank the following: Archives Photographiques, Paris 42; Giraudon 1; F. Lahaye, Maastricht 56; Mansell Collection 11, 36, 83; Marburg 39, 44, 61, 62; Nationalmuseet, Copenhagen IV, V; Yan 58, 70, 71, 72, 76. Illustrations 54 and 55 are from L. T. Belgrano, *Annali Genovesi di Caffaro*, Fonti per la storia d'Italia, vol. I, 1890.